Pastor and Deacons

Biblical Qualifications,
Scriptural Roles,
And Right Relationships

Order this book online at www.trafford.com/07-2827
or email orders@trafford.com

Most Trafford titles are also available at major online book retailers.

© Copyright 2008 John Hartog II.

All rights reserved. No part of this publication may be reproduced, stored in a retrieval system, or transmitted, in any form or by any means, electronic, mechanical, photocopying, recording, or otherwise, without the written prior permission of the author.

Previous Editions Entitled
The Biblical Qualifications of a Pastor
© 1987 & 1992

All scripture quotations, unless otherwise indicated,
are taken from the New King James Version®.
Copyright © 1982 by Thomas Nelson, Inc.
Used by permission.

Some quotations from the New King James Version are additionally marked "NKJV"

References to other versions are noted within the text of this book by their intials:
KJV, NIV, NASB, NEB, NLT or by name: Berkley

Note for Librarians: A cataloguing record for this book is available from Library and Archives Canada at www.collectionscanada.ca/amicus/index-e.html

Printed in Victoria, BC, Canada.

ISBN: 978-1-4251-6201-6

Trafford PUBLISHING

www.trafford.com

North America & international
toll-free: 1 888 232 4444 (USA & Canada)
phone: 250 383 6864 ♦ fax: 250 383 6804
email: info@trafford.com

The United Kingdom & Europe
phone: +44 (0)1865 722 113 ♦ local rate: 0845 230 9601
facsimile: +44 (0)1865 722 868 ♦ email: info.uk@trafford.com

10 9 8 7 6 5 4 3

Pastor and Deacons

Biblical Qualifications,
Scriptural Roles,
And Right Relationships

By

John Hartog II

Trafford Publishing

Word of Thanks

I would like to thank the following people:

My dear wife, Martha, for her long hours of editorial work on each rough draft and her many helpful suggestions, and also for her contributions to chapter 13: "Deaconesses or Deacons' Wives" and Appendix B: "Ministries Open to Women."

Amy Kramer and Mike Griffin for their part in scanning the second edition of *The Biblical Qualifications of a Pastor* so that it could be incorporated into this revised and enlarged edition.

Dr. Earnest Schmidt for checking the first rough draft and for writing the foreword for this edition.

Dorothy Ball for designing the cover.

And my students in New Testament Survey class at Faith Baptist Bible College in Ankeny, Iowa. Their prayers and patience throughout this project sustained me.

Author's Note

As you read *Pastor and Deacons*, you will find quotations from a variety of other works. This is the outcome of my research as I came across the writings of other authors. I have purposely included these quotes to enrich this study and to give credence to the propositions developed in this work.

Dedication

This work is a tribute
to
the memory of
deacon David Lord,
dear friend and fellow laborer,
whose last words to me were,
"Pastor, I love you."

Author's Preface

Every pastor ought to serve as a deacon for ten years before becoming a pastor, and every deacon ought to minister as a pastor for ten years before becoming a deacon.

This, of course, is impossible. However, such a background would help pastors and deacons understand the blessings and challenges related to these two offices. Moreover, this experience would help them appreciate each other better.

I have ministered as a pastor for eleven years in two churches, and I have served as a deacon for eighteen years in three churches. Under the gracious hand of God, I was called upon to open a closed church in the Texas panhandle and later to be the founding pastor of Maranatha Baptist Church in Grimes, Iowa.

The Lord also gave me the privilege of serving as a deacon in First Baptist Church of Lewistown, Montana; Slater Baptist Church of Slater, Iowa; and presently I am a deacon at Faith Baptist Church of Cambridge, Iowa. My service as a deacon has included filling the position of chairman in Slater and Lewistown.

Indeed, God has taught me much as I served in both capacities. This experience with its joys and trials, has prepared me for writing this book on *Pastor and Deacons*. It is my prayer that God will use this effort to help both pastors and deacons meet the Biblical qualifications of their offices. Their compliance to these biblical directives will promote harmony between the pastor and deacons as they minister together in the local church.

Foreword to the second edition

Times have changed. Only a few decades ago pastors were respected for their godliness and discernment. The pastor's knowledge of the Word of God, and the example he set in every day life was an inspiration to those who knew him. Today, the ministry is held up to ridicule. Some men, who stand behind the sacred desk, have sacrificed their testimony for a bowl of worldly pottage. Whether ensnared by lust in immorality, or allured by the riches of this world into financial transgression, such men are biblically disqualified for the ministry.

Dr. John Hartog II has put together in this concise treatment of the primary texts of scripture an exegetically sound and challenging explanation of the pastor's qualifications. He has explained the meaning of each word and phrase that make up the Biblical standard. He has also included a helpful review of the various positions regarding the debated phrase, "the husband of one wife."

Reading the manuscript has been both profitable and encouraging. I commend it to those contemplating pastoral ministry, to pastors who periodically ought to review God's expectations of those in ministry, and to churches who have the responsibility of calling biblical under-shepherds to feed them and lead them into godliness. This world needs a high view of God and a respect for those who are His vocational servants. May God help us to hold fast to the biblical qualifications of a pastor.

Pastor Chris Hindal
Slater Baptist Church
Slater, Iowa
1992

Foreword to the Revised Third Edition

Nothing is more contemporary or relevant than the Bible. Taken by themselves these current "buzzwords" are very short-sighted. From a human standpoint what is contemporary and relevant is extremely temporal. How long before what is now contemporary and relevant is old-fashioned? The plain statements and principles of Scripture are timeless. Psalm 119:89 states, "Forever, O Lord, Your word is settled in Heaven." Our great Eternal God has given us a changeless book to guide our ministries. Any philosophy of ministry and procedures for applying that philosophy should flow from this timeless volume, not from the latest transient fad.

Dr. Hartog's book reflects commitment to and confidence in the Bible's teaching concerning leadership in ministry. Honoring God's Word, he presents the pastor as a shepherd, not a CEO, and deacons as servants/pastor's assistants, not a Board of Directors. Both the qualifications and ministries of these two offices are described from a biblical and practical perspective.

You are about to read a book that is founded upon research and experience. Extensive quotes from exegetical, expositional, and practical literature put a wealth of information in compact form, as well as exposing the reader to sources for further study. Dr. Hartog presents the various interpretative approaches to significant biblical statements and issues. He then helps you think through the material so you can come to legitimate conclusions.

This volume is not written from an academic ivory tower. Dr. Hartog has "been there." In the right sense of the term, he has successfully served as both a pastor and deacon. The biblical lists of qualifications for these offices stress character, not just skills. Our author exemplifies peerless character. He personally lives what he describes. His family also demonstrates his character. They not only rise up and call him blessed, they reflect a home life described in 1 Timothy 3 and Titus 1.

Every believer should read this book. The qualifications describe the type of people churches should be growing to supply the need for present and future leaders. As you read, be prepared to be convicted and challenged. Most importantly, read it to be changed.

Dr. Ernie Schmidt
Academic Dean
Faith Baptist
Theological
Seminary
Ankeny,
Iowa

Table of Contents

	Page
Dedication	7
Author's Preface	9
Foreword to the 2nd Edition	11
Foreword to the 3rd Revised Edition	13
Contents	15
An Opening Word	17
Chapter 1: Dictators in the church	19

Part One: The Office of Pastor — 25

Chapter 2: Introduction to the Office of Pastor	27
Chapter 3: What a Pastor Should Not Be	31
Chapter 4: What a Pastor Should Be	43
Chapter 5: The Pastor and His Family	53
Chapter 6: The Pastor and Others	65
Chapter 7: The Pastor's Reward	71

Part Two: The Office of Deacons — 75

Chapter 8: Were "the Seven" Deacons or Not?	77
Chapter 9: Introduction to Office of Deacons	81
Chapter 10: The Chosen Few of Acts 6	87

Contents (Continued)

	Page
Chapter 11: What a Deacon Should Not Be	93
Chapter 12: What a Deacon Should Be	101
Chapter 13: Deaconesses or Deacons' Wives?	109
Chapter 14: The Deacon and His Family	121
Chapter 15: What Deacons' Wives Should Be	127
Chapter 16: The Deacons' Reward for Serving Well	133

| ***Part Three: Roles and Relationships*** | **137** |
| ***of the Pastor and Deacons*** | |

Chapter 17: The Pastor's Scriptural Roles	139
Chapter 18: The Deacons' Scriptural Role	155
Chapter 19: Right Relationships	161

| ***Appendices*** | **165** |

Appendix A: "A Tribute to Pastors"	167
Appendix B: "And What about Women?"	179
"Ministries Open to Women"	181
Scripture References	187
Selected Bibliography	193

An Opening Word

The basic premise upon which this book rests is that the Bible is the guiding principle that gives direction for the organization and operation of the local church. 2 Timothy 3:16-17 states, "All Scripture is given by inspiration of God, and is profitable for doctrine, for reproof, for correction, for instruction in righteousness, that the man of God may be complete, thoroughly equipped for every good work." Thus, every pastor and deacon should be a "man of God," one who is mature and prepared for "every good work."

The inspired Word gives the qualifications which both the pastor and deacons should meet, and it also sheds light on their roles. Moreover, in the Scriptures we find principles that bear upon the relationship that should exist between those who hold these two offices.

In our study we will seek to be Biblically sound. We believe that the Bible is our only authority for faith and practice, and we reflect this belief in our Baptist Distinctives:

B ible Our Only Authority
A utomomy of the Local Church
P riesthood of All Believers
T wo Offices: Pastor and Deacons
I mmersed, Regenerated Membership
S oul Liberty
T wo Ordinances: Baptism and Communion
S eparation of Church and State

The first distinctive, the "Bible our only authority" will dictate our method in this important undertaking. The fourth distinctive, "Two Offices: Pastor and Deacons," is the emphasis of this endeavor.

Chapter 1

DICTATORS IN THE CHURCH

In his third epistle, the apostle John wrote to Gaius concerning a man who has come down in history as the first "church boss." John says, "I wrote to the church, but Diotrephes, who loves to have the preeminence among them, does not receive us. Therefore, if I come, I will call to mind his deeds which he does, prating against us with malicious words. And not content with that, he himself does not receive the brethren, and forbids those who wish to, putting them out of the church" (vv. 9-10).

Diotrephes wanted to be the boss of that early apostolic local church, and he did not care what anyone else thought, not even the apostle John!

In 1893, A. T. Robertson wrote an article on Diotrephes for a denominational magazine. The article created quite a stir. Twenty-five angry deacons wrote the editor of the magazine to cancel their subscriptions. These deacons thought that the magazine was attacking them personally![1] (If the shoe fits . . . !) Dictators in the church come in all sizes and shapes, and they may be either men or women.

Women Dictators

One Sunday I filled the pulpit in a church because its pastor was out of town for the day. When I arrived at the church, a lady who looked to be in her eighties met me at the door. Her first words to me were, "I run this church." It took me back for a moment, but as the day wore on, I came to realize that she really did run the church.

Before any decision was made, it had to have the approval of "Nelly" (Her name has been changed to protect the guilty party). Her word was the last word regarding which songs the congregation would sing, who would lead the morning service, who should bring flowers for decorations the next week, etc. As the "matron saint" of the congregation, she really did "run the church," and she was unashamedly open about it.

Sometimes the strong-willed wife of a meek and mild deacon gives out orders. She pulls the strings from behind the scenes, but she is just as much the dictator of the church.

Pastor Dictator

This is the type of pastor who rules with an iron hand. He is the empire builder, and the church is his kingdom. An extreme example of such a case is one I read about in a message on the relationship between a pastor and the deacons.

In this message the speaker repeatedly called the deacons "errand boys." He stated that their task was to "go out and get the groceries." According to him, the deacons were the root of the problems in churches. He proclaimed that "90% of the trouble in the churches has arrived because of the perverted doctrine of deacons."[2]

But that was not all the speaker said! He went on to declare, "The pastor is the overseer of every department. He is the one who gives the orders, not the one who takes them from the deacons (errand boys). The deacons' job is to run those errands; the pastor's job is to rule the church. God puts the blue prints in the hands of the pastor and says, 'Here is what I want you to do.' Then some pastors take a week to figure out what kind of psychology [to use] to present it to the 'board.' Think of it. The leader asking the followers if it is alright to do what God says. Think of it. The Overseer, the leader, God's representative, asking some cigarette [smoking], lodge-member, clock-watching, Hollywood-loving, out of order, carnal church members, if it is alright to do what God told him to do. How far from the Word of God can a preacher and a church get? Hodge-podge 'Fundamentalism!'"[3]

Recently I saw a cartoon of a pastor leading a deacons' meeting making this announcement: "From now on we're going to operate as a theocracy . . . and I'm Theo."[4] Definitely no pastor should ever go that route. It is, of course, true that the pastor is the overseer of the church. That is biblical. Nonetheless, no pastor, no shepherd of the flock, should have this view of the deacons. God calls pastors to be leaders, not to be dictators. The apostle Peter dealt with this issue and exhorted the elders to "shepherd" the flock of God, serving as "overseers," not as "lords," but as "examples" to the flock (1 Pet. 5:3). Thus, a pastor is not to lord it over his congregation but is to feed it God's Word and lead it gently through his exemplary life.

Deacon Dictator

This type of deacon will often oppose everything that the pastor brings up. He acquires a sense of power when he can convince the other deacons to side with him against the pastor.

Anything that is not this deacon's own idea is something against which to rally the troops. This deacon is domineering, and the other deacons often fall in line behind him just to "keep the peace." He speaks up on every issue and usually ends up being the "chairman of the deacon board." From this position he can throw his weight around even more.

Frequently this type of deacon dictator is one who loudly proclaims that the pastor is a dictator. O'Donnell warns against deacon dictators when he writes, "When a pastor is elected as the leader in the church, deacons need to recognize the leadership of the pastor and follow him. In many of our churches [Free Will Baptist] across the land, strong deacon leadership has continued after churches have called full-time pastors. Deacons in these churches continue to dominate the church regardless of who is called as pastor. Such churches become known for the rapid turnover in its [sic. their] pastors. Usually a pastor can serve only until his policies come in conflict with the dominant deacon. Then he has to move."[5]

I know of one church that has the reputation of being a "pastor killer" church. This church has had an ongoing turnover of both its pastors and its people. The membership is down to six or eight people, but the church still has its deacon dictator. Beware of any deacon who always opposes the pastor—any pastor that the church might call. "A church family, like a family, are loyal to one another, and deacons owe a particular loyalty to the pastor."[6]

Jackson points out the devastating results of not complying with the pastoral leadership ordained by God. He says, "Many churches have been torn apart because some deacon, or deacons, misunderstood the divine order in this matter, and became dictatorial, assuming authority the Lord never gave."[7]

God's plan for the church is different. The Bible clearly lays out the Biblical qualifications and roles of both pastors and deacons. God wants them to follow their Scriptural roles. Doing so promotes unity, which is God's will and desire for His church. When differences of opinion threaten the unity of the church, pastors and deacons must strive towards a biblical consensus in a God-honoring manner. "People who know they are secure in God's hand find their motives shaped in that awareness. They learn to live with grace, to disagree in kindness, to love freely, and to trust God from day to day when matters beyond their control do not go their way."[8]

All of us, especially pastors and deacons, must obey Paul's exhortation to the Philippian congregation: "Let nothing be done through selfish ambition or conceit, but in lowliness of mind let each esteem others better than himself" (Philippians 2:3).

NOTES FOR
CHAPTER ONE

[1] A. T, Robertson, *Word Pictures in the New Testament* (Nashville, TN: Broadman Press, 1933), p. 263.

[2] Robert J. Terry, *Pastoral Leadership* (Plymouth, MN: Plymouth Baptist Church, 1974), p. 46, citing Evangelist Bob Oughton, "Open Bible Times." Volume 3, Number 6, June 1965

[3] Ibid., p. 44.

[4] Harold J. Westing, *Church Staff Handbook*, rev. ed. (Grand Rapids, MI: Kregel Publications, 1997), p. 29.

[5] J. D. O'Donnell, *Handbook for Deacons* (Nashville TN: Randall House Publications, 1973), pp. 54-55.

[6] David A. Norris, *Congregational Harmony: A Manual for Deacons and Church Workers*, rev. ed. (Ames, IA: Church Strengthening Ministries, 1984), p.16.

[7] Paul R. Jackson, *The Doctrine and Administration of the Church* (Schaumburg, IL: Regular Baptist Press, 1980), p. 42.

[8] David Sper, editor. *How Can We Work Through Our Differences* (Grand Rapids: Resources for Biblical Communication, 1992), p. 9.

Part One

The Office of Pastor

Chapter 2

INTRODUCTION TO THE OFFICE OF PASTOR

Ben came to Bible college from his home on the ranch. He loved the wide open spaces, and he thought that this was where he would spend his life. However, Ben also wanted to learn more about the Bible, so he decided to attend Bible college for a school year. One year away from the ranch would not be so long, and soon he would be back home on the range!

Ben was a good student. God had given him a keen mind, and he studied diligently. As the school year came to a close, Ben decided to continue his studies and complete four years toward a bachelor's degree. Then, he could return to the ranch. After all, he would still have many years left after graduation.

A New Direction

The years passed quickly. Ben learned Bible, theology, some Greek, and church history. At Bible college he met Mary, a wonderful Christian girl, whom

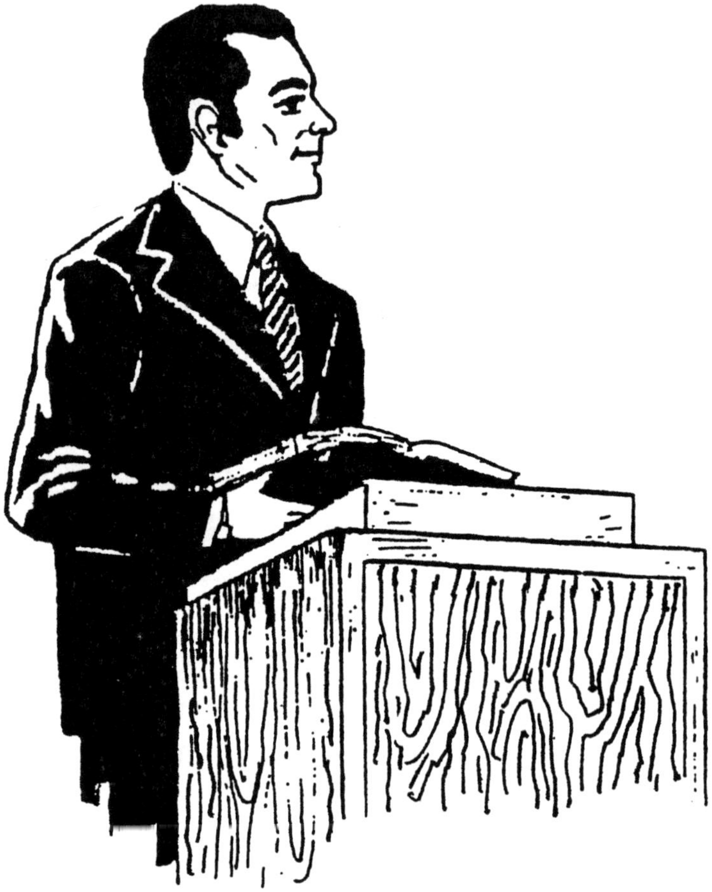

he married after graduation. During his senior year, Ben thought much about the ranch and his future. As he prayed and searched the Scriptures, he became convinced that God was calling him to a different vocation in life. God wanted him to be a pastor.

Ben said, "Yes!" to God's call, and he spent several more years in seminary preparing to be the best pastor that he could be. Ben—along with Mary, his wife and loyal helper—has been a great blessing to his church community. His faithful preaching of the Word of God has changed many lives. May the Lord call more godly men like Ben to shepherd our churches!

What does it take to be a godly pastor? Who is qualified to be one? What does the Bible teach concerning this important office? Let us seek to answer these questions.

The Biblical Terms

In the New Testament, three Greek words refer to a pastor. Following are these words and brief meanings: (1) *poimen*, "pastor," speaks of his care for the flock as he feeds them God's Word and protects them from false teaching; (2) *episkopos*, "bishop," emphasizes his role to oversee the ministries of the local church; and (3) *presbuteros*, "elder," relates to the pastor's spiritual, emotional, mental, and physical maturity.

"The parallel descriptions of qualifications for *bishop* (or overseer) in 1 Timothy 3 and for *elder* in Titus 1 suggest that these two terms, along with *shepherd, presbyter*, and *pastor*, are synonymous."[1] In addition, 1 Peter 5:1 uses the word *sumpresbuteros* translated "fellow-elder."

The Biblical Passages

These biblical terms occur in fifteen chapters of eight New Testament books: (Acts 11, 14, 15, 16, 20, 21, 22; Eph. 4; Phil. 1; 1 Tim. 3, 5; Tit. 1; 1 Pet. 5; 2 Pet. 2; and James 5). Of these fifteen chapters, only two give a list of qualifications of the pastor. They are 1Timothy 3 and Titus 1. These two chapters list about two dozen qualifications. Some are found in both chapters and some are found only in one or the other. Some are positive and some are negative.

Lets us now embark on a study of the Biblical requirements of a pastor!

NOTES FOR CHAPTER TWO

[1] Larry Richards, *Pass It On: Our Heritage from the Apostolic Age: Studies to 1 and 2 Timothy, Titus, 1 and 2 Peter, Jude, 1, 2, and 3 John* (Elgin, IL: David C. Cook Publishing Co., 1978), pp. 42-43.

Chapter 3

WHAT A PASTOR SHOULD NOT BE

Considering what something *is not*, sometimes helps us understand what something *is*. Thus, we will begin with the negative qualifications for pastors listed in the New Testament. These are undesirable traits in any individual, so since the pastoral vocation is a high and holy calling, a pastor certainly should guard against these ungodly characteristics. Moreover, God's Word exhorts him to be an example to the flock (1 Pet. 5:3).

Not Blamable

Anepilempton (1 Tim. 3:2). A pastor must be a man who is irreproachable. The negative aspect of this qualification does not come through so clearly in either the KJV or the NKJV, which say, "A bishop then must be blameless." A literal translation of this phrase, "A bishop then must **not** be blamable," shows that this is a negative characteristic.

Kent explains this when he writes, "The adjective *anepilempton* is derived from *lambano*, *epi*, 'upon,' and the alpha privative which negates the quality."[1] Thus a pastor must be one who cannot be taken hold upon; that is, he must be irreproachable.

The synonym *anegkleton* of Titus 1:7 teaches the same thing about a bishop. This synonym also means blameless. He must be one whose life is characterized by "unimpeachable uprightness."[2] The reason is because "He acts as God's steward (*oikonomos*; NIV, 'entrusted with God's work')."[3]

Blameless does not mean sinless perfection. "Do not misunderstand. The Apostle does not mean that a bishop must be sinless. If so, we could not have any bishops."[4] Sinless perfection is not attainable in this life by any pastor or layman. We will never reach that point until we receive our glorified bodies.

Moreoever, it does not mean that a pastor must resign from his pulpit if anyone in the church or outside of it blames him for the troubles in the church. "The thing that must be understood is that you *will* be blamed for things if you hold an office, any office, in the church. What is important is that the accusation must not be true. An elder must be blameless in the sense that he will not be found guilty of anything that he might be accused of."[5] (Italics in original). The word *blameless* describes a person who is "morally careful and responsible"[6]

Not a Recent Convert

Me neophuton (1 Tim. 3:6). A pastor should not be a novice. This word means newly planted or newly converted.[7] The New English Bible mistranslates this

"And to think
I've only been
saved six months!"

phrase as "a convert newly baptized." It is not a question of baptism. The point is that the pastoral candidate should not be a recent convert for that could make him also a candidate for pride—the very sin into which the devil fell soon after his creation.

Turning this negative quality into a positive one shows us clearly that Paul's injunction is that a man who desires to be a pastor must be, first of all, a mature Christian, not a new babe in Christ. Maturity comes with time, knowledge of God's Word, and living in light of that knowledge.

What did Paul mean when he said, "lest being lifted up with pride he fall into the condemnation of the devil?" (1 Tim. 3:6b KJV). One view is that this immature pastor will be cast into hell like the devil ultimately will be.[8] However, the Biblical teaching of eternal security rules out this view.

A second view is that the devil will condemn the novice pastor. That is, the devil as God's agent inflicts punishment on the pastor.[9] While the book of Job may give some basis for this view, the context does not go along with that of Job at all. The problem with this pastor is the sin of pride, while Job was an upright man.

A third theory is that Satan's agents (i.e., unsaved people) will condemn this pastor, and their condemnation would ruin his witness for Christ. This reads something into the text that is not there.

A fourth view is that this novice pastor, because of his pride, will incur punishment for sin just like the devil incurred punishment for his sin of pride (thus, "as the devil" in the NKJV). Pride was the first sin of the devil, and he became useless to God. A novice who becomes a pastor and falls into pride will not be effective for Christ. "As Satan lost his princely standing by pride and rebellion, so also is the new believer especially vulnerable to failure and remorse if elevated to leadership so quickly that it will go to his head."[10]

Not Covetous

Aphilarguron (1 Tim. 3:3). Likewise, a pastor should not be covetous. The Greek word has an alpha privative (the first a of *aphilarguron* negates the word) and means literally "not a lover of silver." We live in a materialistic age in which covetousness is a prevalent temptation. The love of money has not faded with the passing of the centuries. Whether a pastor receives a sizable salary or a meager one, the temptation to want more and more of this world's goods may be the same. However, "the overseer is not to have his attention fixed upon the monetary rewards."[11]

Not Greedy for Money

Me aischrokerde (Tit. 1:7). Note that this characteristic from the list in Titus is similar to the one just above from the list in 1 Timothy. The NEB translates this expression picturesquely as, "no money-grabber." The phrase literally rendered is "not fond of sordid gain." This same qualification is required of a deacon in 1 Timothy 3:8. The pastor and deacons oversee the finances of the church, and the temptation of embezzlement is always present.

The pastor "is not to use his office as a means for the accumulation of unjust gain."[12] The ministry should never be considered a money-making business, and no one should be in it for the salary he earns from it. Unfortunately, sometimes money is the top priority, and the salary dictates the acceptance of a pastoral call. A pastor who is constantly occupied with amassing money will be too preoccupied to feed his people.

At the time of this writing, our newspaper had an article about a pastor who fell into the evil of gambling. He even gambled away some funds of the church. Moreover, He caused his family great grief; he left behind a disillusioned membership; and the church removed him from the pastorate. I know of another area pastor who habitually took money out of the offering before it was counted. His congregation also asked him to leave.

A pastor should not count the offerings; he certainly must not count them alone. He should insist that at least two individuals working together always count, record, and initial the church's donations. My policy as a pastor was to remain unaware of what each individual member contributed.

Not Self-willed

Me authade (Tit. 1:7). "This adjective is derived from *hedomai*, enjoy oneself, take pleasure, and *autos*, self."[13] The word speaks of one who is self-pleasing, self-willed, arrogant (RSV), or overbearing (NIV, NEB). Here Paul teaches us that a pastor should not be a headstrong, stubborn man who seeks to gratify himself in arrogant disregard of others. A man who always wants his own way, regardless of the wishes or the advice of others, has no place in the pastorate.

Not Quick-tempered

Me orgilon (Tit. 1:7). The overseer must not be quick-tempered. This is the only time in the New Testament that the word *orgilon* appears, although its cognates are frequent. A man who has a hot temper is just as disqualified from the pastorate as a man who is a drunkard. A pastor should not be short-tempered because much of his work in the ministry is with his people, and working with people requires patience.

Someone has said, "Temper is such a wonderful thing that it's a shame to lose it."[14] Of itself, anger can be a good thing. A righteous man ought to be angry against injustices and be indignant because of the "wicked who forsake God's law" (Ps. 119:53). The Bible contains many examples of God's anger against His people when they sin. He was angry with sinning Israel for forty years, and their corpses fell in the wilderness (Heb 3:17).

Not a Drunkard

Me paroinon (1 Tim. 3:3; Tit. 1:7). A pastor should not be a drunkard. A literal translation of this phrase is "one who does not come along side of wine." The NASB has the expression as "not addicted to wine."

The KJV/NKJV rendering, "not given to wine," is slightly changed in wording but greatly changed in implication by the NIV which translates it, "not given to much wine." This would allow for a pastor to indulge in some drinking, such as social drinking, as long as he did not overdue it. Conrad says, "The term does not prohibit occasional use of wine."[15] Guthrie says that *given to wine* implies drunkenness and that "such excesses are clearly quite alien to the Christian Spirit."[16] Green concurs, "Concerning wine, Paul's instruction to a bishop is very clear. He is not to participate in such practice."[17]

Hughes describes the days of the apostolic church as "rough and tumble." He writes, "drunkenness was an ancient blight. . . . Some Christians were even in the habit of getting drunk at the Lord's Supper (cf. 1 Corinthians 11:21)! Paul repeats this warning to deacons in verse 8 . . . and again to elders in Titus 1:7. . . . This must be taken to heart today by church leaders in a culture that romanticizes drinking. . . . The real truth is, alcohol is a destroyer of truth."[18]

Not a Fighter

Me plekten (1 Tim. 3:3; Tit. 1:7). A man who gets drunk usually will get into fights as well. In 1 Timothy and in Titus, the admonition that a bishop should not be given to wine precedes another one, which states that he should not be a combatant. The KJV translates this phrase as "no striker" and the NKJV has "not violent." The Greek words literally mean "not pugnacious" as the NASB renders them. The Berkley version renders it graphically, "not a fist-fighter." A pastor must not be one who is eager and ready to fight. He should leave his boxing gloves behind when he enters the ministry!

Regretfully, throughout its history, the Church has had its share of violent pastors. "A certain pastor got into an argument with his deacon and in the heated argument knocked the deacon down, and thereby he knocked himself out of his church and all influence in the community."[19] A pastor who is given over to acts of bodily violence certainly brings harm not only to others, but most importantly to the cause of Christ. Such a man is biblically disqualified from the pastoral ministry.

Not Quarrelsome

Amachon (1 Tim. 3:3). This Greek word again has an alpha privative and is translated negatively in the KJV as "not a brawler." The NEB translates the previous qualification *me plekten* (not a fighter) as, "not quarrelsome." However, *amachon* and *me plekten* are obviously two different Greek terms. *Amachon* is better rendered "uncontentious," or, as the NKJV has it, "not quarrelsome." Its opposite is "conciliatory."

We saw earlier that a pastor must refrain from physical fights. He also must stay clear of verbal fights. Trentham describes a person who displays a quarrelsome spirit as "the man who lacks courage to face a member of his congregation forthrightly and personally with his accusations against him, choosing rather to hide his cowardice behind a pulpit and striking when the worshiper cannot strike back."[20]

However, a pastor should not strike even if the worshiper could strike back and must not be offensively aggressive. He may properly debate theological matters, but must keep his temper under control. He should seek to exhibit love and peace, which are aspects of the fruit of the Spirit. A pastor certainly must speak up and "contend earnestly for the faith which was once delivered to the saints" (Jude v. 3), but he must do it in a loving manner just as Paul commanded (Eph. 4:15).

NOTES FOR
CHAPTER THREE

[1] Homer A. Kent, Jr., *The Pastoral Epistles: Studies in I and II Timothy and Titus* (Chicago: Moody Press, 1958), p. 121.

[2] E. M. Blaiklock, *The Pastoral Epistles* (Grand Rapids: Zondervan Publishing House, 1972), p. 76.

[3] Walter L. Liefield, *1 & 2 Timothy, Titus* in *The NIV Application Commentary* (Grand Rapids: Zondervan, 1999), p. 313.

[4] H. A. Ironside, *Addresses on the First and Second Epistles of Timothy, Also Lectures on the Epistle to Titus* (New York: Loizeaux Brothers, 1947), p. 77.

[5] J. Vernon McGee, *I Timothy, II Timothy, Titus, and Philemon* (Pasadena, CA: Thru the Bible Books, 1978), p. 52.

[6] Liefeld, *1 & 2 Timothy, Titus*, p. 118.

[7] Dean Fetterhoff, *The Making of a Man of God: Studies in 1 & 2 Timothy* (Winona Lake, IN: BMH Books, 1976), p 53.

[8] Omar Gregory Conrad, "A Teacher's Manual for the Book of First Timothy," MABS thesis (Dallas: Dallas Theological Seminary, 1977), p. 49.

[9] A. T. Hanson, *The Pastoral Epistles* (Grand Rapids: Wm. B. Eerdmans Publishing Co., 1982), p. 76.

[10] Robert H. Mounce, *Pass It On: First and Second Timothy* (Glendale, CA: G. L. Regal Books, 1979), p. 40.

[11] Kent, *Pastoral Epistles*, p. 128.

[12] Edmond Hiebert, *Titus and Philemon* (Chicago: Moody Press, 1957), p. 34.

[13] Kent, *Pastoral Epistles*, p. 214.

[14] Warren W. Wiersbe, *Be Faithful, It's Always too Soon to Quit! An Expository Study of the Pastoral Epistles, 1 and 2 Timothy and Titus* (Wheaton, IL: Victor Books, 1981), p. 101.

[15] Conrad, "Teacher's Manual," p. 48

[16] Donald Guthrie, *The Pastoral Epistles: An Introduction and Commentary* (Grand Rapids: Wm. B. Eerdmans Publishing Co., 1957), p. 81.

[17] Oliver B. Greene, *The Epistles of Paul the Apostle to Timothy and Titus* (Greenville, SC: The Gospel Hour, Inc., 1964), p. 114.

[18] R. Kent Hughes, and Bryan Chapell, *1 & 2 Timothy and Titus: To Guard the Deposit* (Wheaton, IL: Crossway Books, 2000), p. 80.

[19] Hiebert, *Titus and Philemon*, p. 34.

[20] Charles A. Trentham, *Studies in Timothy* (Nashville: Convention Press, 1959), p. 40.

Chapter 4

WHAT A PASTOR SHOULD BE

By itself, freedom from undesirable traits does not qualify a man to be a pastor. In 1 Timothy 3 and Titus 1, the Apostle Paul listed eight positive characteristics that a person must possess in order to meet the requirements of the pastoral office. The forsaking of ungodly traits and putting on Christ-like qualities is a biblical principle (cf. Rom. 13:12-14; Eph. 4:17-32; Col. 3:5-17). Therefore, a pastor must also clothe himself with some godly qualities that will enable him to fulfill his ministry.

Temperate

Nephalion (1 Tim. 3:2). This word, translated "vigilant" in the KJV, comes from a Greek root related to the word "head" and can be paraphrased "clear-headed." It is often rendered as "sober" or "temperate" as in the NKJV and NASB. Originally this word meant total abstinence from alcohol, which would reinforce the earlier statement that an overseer should not drink at all.

Since Paul mentions abstinence from wine late in his list, he probably used the term here in the wider sense of sobriety of judgment. Of course, a man under the influence of alcohol is not sober in judgment either. A pastor must be sober in judgment in order to avoid falling prey to the attacks of Satan and to false teaching. "He is to be a man sober and fully rational, in possession of the full use of all his faculties."[1]

Sober-minded

Sophrona (1 Tim. 3:2; Tit. 1:8). "Prudent" is an accurate translation for this word. It comes from two Greek words that mean *sane* and *mind*. *Sophrona* describes someone who is sane in both judgment and behavior; and it pictures a man who is well-balanced, composed, and discreet, with a properly regulated mind. A pastor should not be "light and frivolous, but serious, discreet, and sober in deportment."[2]

Kent explains the importance of this adjective: It "is a quality of mind which is serious, earnest, sound. It does not mean the minister should be long faced, but he should be earnest. . . . The overseer, especially if he is young, must avoid the reputation of a clown. Young people may think such a preacher is funny, but they won't come to him for spiritual help."[3] Prudence "requires humor and fun to be kept in balance. What a man laughs at shows something about what he is."[4]

Well-ordered

Cosmion (1 Tim. 3:2). "Of good behavior" (KJV and NKJV). *Cosmion* is used in classical Greek and in the inscriptions to describe a person as "orderly, well behaved, or virtuous."[5] "Respectable" is a literal translation. A pastor should be a man of dignity.

"Whatever makes
you think that
a pastor needs
the gift of administration
and be
well organized?"

The word *cosmetic* comes from the same Greek root. Cosmetics are used to bring out the beauty in a person's outward appearance. An overseer should also be concerned with his life style as others see him. His manner of living should adorn the gospel.

This adjective, *cosmion*, is a cognate of the Greek word *cosmeo*, which means "to arrange." God is a God of order, and the cosmos that He created is not a chaos. It is an orderly arrangement of heavenly bodies. Every aspect of the pastor's life should reflect this orderly structure, including his sermons—they should be well organized. "The ministry is no place for the man whose life is a continual confusion of unaccomplished plans and unorganized activity."[6]

Gentle

Epieike (1 Tim. 3:3). The KJV renders this word as "patient." Literally it means "gentle" as found in the NKJV. Kelly uses the word "magnanimous," and he explains its meaning as "the gracious condescension, or forbearingness, with which the Christian pastor should deal with his charges, however exasperating they may on occasion be."[7] He should follow Christ's example who embodies perfect gentleness. He said of Himself, "I am gentle and lowly in heart" (Mat. 11:29, cf. 2 Cor. 10:1).

2 Timothy 2:24-25 gives a detailed description of this beautiful quality. This is how Paul depicted it to Timothy: "And the Lord's servant must not quarrel; instead, he must be kind to everyone, able to teach, not resentful. Those who oppose him he must gently instruct, in the hope that God will grant them repentance leading them to a knowledge of the truth." Gentleness is also an aspect of the fruit of the Spirit (Gal. 5:22-23).

Just

Dikaion (Tit. 1:8). Another translation of this word is "upright" or "righteous." This qualification and the next one, *osion*, are similar. Kent prefers "just" or "righteousness" as a translation for *dikaion*. He believes that it "refers to conduct which meets the approval of God. The term is a legal one, and here refers to the verdict as pronounced by the divine Judge."[8]

Hiebert maintains that this quality refers to the pastor's proper dealings with his fellow men. He says, "His conduct in relation to others must conform to the standard of right. Any minister who is not upright in all his dealings with his fellow men can do little good."[9] Greene also sees this word in that light. He speaks of the fact that a pastor "must be honest, upright, open and above board in all his dealings with his fellow man."[10] Perhaps both views are true, and the word speaks of the pastor's relationship to God and also to mankind.

Holy

Osion (Tit. 1:8) translated "devout" contains the idea of being pure, unpolluted, and unstained by sin. *Osion* "is used here of one who is 'devout, pious, pleasing to God."[11] If the word "just" above refers more to the pastor's duty to his neighbor, this word "holy" relates more to his duty to God. Like all believers, a pastor should be holy because God is holy (1 Pet. 1:16).

Self-controlled

Egkrate (Tit. 1:8). The KJV renders this word "temperate," but that is somewhat confusing because temperate is also a viable translation of *nephalion*, which is the first qualification listed in this chapter. The NKJV translation "self-controlled" for *egkrate* is preferable. This word comes from a root meaning "to hold, or seize" and the word for "in." Thus, the idea is to hold in check or to restrain. An overseer must be a man who controls both his appetites and his actions. In explaining why a pastor should be self-controlled, Wiersbe makes this amusing but truthful point: "He must discipline his desires, especially when well-meaning members try to stuff him with coffee and cake!"[12]

Doctrinally Sound

Antechomenon tou kata ten didachen pistou logou (Tit. 1:9). This expression describes the doctrinal qualification of the overseer, and it may be rendered "holding to the faithful word which is according to the teaching." A pastor must "know and be zealously committed to the apostolic teaching and willing to teach it and to rebuke those who oppose it."[13]

Some downplay doctrine; their slogan is "doctrine divides but love unites." This is not biblical. A church that has a sound doctrinal statement, which its members firmly believe and practice, will be a strong, united congregation. A church that is fuzzy in its doctrine is the target of every new fad that happens to come along. Unsound doctrine leads to splinter groups that destroy the unity of the church community and scatter the sheep in all directions! In contrast, sound doctrine unites and keeps the sheep in the same fold! Doctrinal stability must characterize the overseer of the congregation. He must imitate Timothy, who had carefully followed Paul's doctrine (2 Tim. 3:19).

The phrase "faithful saying" appears several times in the Pastoral Epistles. Each time Paul uses it, he connects it with some important doctrine (cf. 1 Tim. 1:15; 3:1; 4:9; 2 Tim. 2:11; Tit. 3:8). God's written Word is inspired by the Holy Spirit; thus it is faithful.

"*Tou kata ten didachen*" literally rendered is "the one according to the teaching." Three views exist among commentators concerning the meaning of this phrase.

(1) Some who follow the NKJV rendering, "as he has been taught," take this to mean that the pastor must hold on to the teaching that was imparted to him. Within our culture, this means that a pastor should not forsake what his teachers taught him in Bible college and seminary. This is good advice as long as he received sound biblical training.

(2) "Others have suggested the meaning to be that he should hold to the 'faithful word in his teaching' (that is, in his own teaching ministry)."[14] In today's setting, as a pastor preaches or teaches, he needs to make sure that his sermons or lessons are true to God's Word. This, too, is good advice.

(3) Some think that the phrase, "holding to the faithful word which is according to the teaching" means that a pastor must hold to God's Word in accordance with the whole body of truth as taught by the apostles. "The statement presupposes the existence of a body of Christian teaching which, in substance if not in form, was already fixed. To this Word, reliable and worthy of utmost confidence, the bishop must resolutely cling if he is to fulfill his function."[15]

A twenty-first century pastor should not seek to come up with some new, undiscovered teaching that supposedly has been hidden behind the words of Scripture for nearly two millennia of church history!

Paul then gives two reasons why a pastor must be correct in doctrine. First, "that he may be able, by sound doctrine . . . to exhort." The word "exhort" conveys the meaning of "comfort" or "coming along side of" someone. The pastor must encourage, admonish, feed, and strengthen the sheep. This pastoral care should come in the area of "sound doctrine," which "means 'healthful' teaching, and so stands in direct contrast to the sickly, morbid, and unpractical teaching of the false teachers."[16]

A second reason why the pastor must be doctrinally sound is so that he may be able "to convict those who contradict" (NKJV) or "convince the gainsayers" (KJV). These are people who oppose the truth. "To convict" is more than simply to reprove; "to refute" is a better expression. The pastor is to know the Bible so well that his convictions are strongly anchored in God's Word. Then his teaching will thoroughly demolish and prove baseless the arguments of those who oppose God's truth.

A man who desires the office of a pastor must meet these biblical qualities, and every church must require them of its pastor. "In admitting a man to the ministry the primary consideration must ever be the integrity of his character rather than his spectacular gifts. No intellectual power or pulpit brilliancy can atone for the lack of solid Christian virtues and blameless life."[17]

**NOTES FOR
CHAPTER FOUR**

---

[1] D. Edmond Hiebert, *First Timothy* (Chicago: Moody Press, 1957), p. 65.

[2] Hiebert, *Titus and Philemon*, p. 35.

[3] Kent, *Pastoral Epistles*, p. 127.

[4] Douglas R. McLachlan, "The Marks of Leadership: I Timothy 3:1-7," Class notes (Minneapolis: Central Baptist Theological Seminary, 1986), p. 30.

[5] George W. Knight, III, *Commentary on the Pastoral Epistles* in *New International Greek Testament Commentary* (Grand Rapids: Eerdmans Publishing Co., 1992), p. 159.

[6] Kent, *Pastoral Epistles*, p. 127.

[7] J. N. D. Kelly, *A Commentary on the Pastoral Epistles* (Grand Rapids: Baker Book House, 1981), p. 77.

[8] Kent, *Pastoral Epistles*, p. 215.

[9] Hiebert, *Titus and Philemon*, p. 35.

[10] Oliver B. Greene, *The Epistles of Paul*, p. 418.

[11] Knight, *Commentary on the Pastoral Epistles*, p. 292.

[12] Wiersbe, *Be Faithful*, p. 102.

[13] Knight, *Commentary on the Pastoral Epistles*, p. 294.

[14] Kent, *Pastoral Epistles*, p. 215.

[15] Hiebert, *Titus and Philemon*, p. 36.

[16] Ibid.

[17] Hiebert, *Titus and Philemon*, p. 37.

Chapter 5

THE PASTOR AND HIS FAMILY

Thus far we have studied nine undesirable qualities that should not characterize a pastor, followed by eight desirable ones, which he should possess. Together these qualities give a clear picture of what a pastor should and should not be. Now we must consider how a pastor should relate to others. We will study him in relation to his family, his congregation, and his community.

According to the Bible, the pastor's relationship to his wife and his children is crucial. A man who is free from the negative traits and who displays the positive ones may still not qualify for the pastorate. It is possible that his behavior in the home does not correspond with his conduct in public. In our day, the most controversial area of all of the ministerial qualifications concerns the pastor's relationship to his wife.

The Pastor and His Wife

Mias gunaikos andra (1 Tim. 3:2; Tit. 1:6). The KJV and NKJV translate this as "the husband of one wife." The Greek is without the definite article, and thus we have here a qualitative expression. The emphasis is on the word "one," and the phrase literally translated is "a one-woman man." Clearly this means that a pastor must be monogamous, which should settle the whole matter. However, that is far from the case. The meaning of this important phrase has been a debatable issue since early church history. Let us examine some of the proposed views.

1. Exclusion of Unmarried Pastors

Some believe that according to this phrase, "the husband of one wife," the apostle was excluding all unmarried men from the pastorate. Or, to turn it around, only married men are eligible for the office. Just a few Bible commentators actually hold this view. Kent states that he was unable to find anyone who actually held it.[1] However, in the past, two men leaned toward this view: Oliver B. Greene and J. Vernon McGee. Both of these men led Christian radio programs, and they also authored numerous books.

Oliver B. Greene, in commenting on this verse, states, "I believe with all my heart that Paul is also saying here that a man appointed to the office of bishop should be a man, a *married man* (with one wife) . . . I believe verse 5 *proves* that a bishop or deacon should be married—the husband of a wife and head of a household"[2] (Italics his).

Greene adds, "It is my conviction that a man placed in the office of bishop, deacon—or in the capacity of leadership, regardless of the title of the office—should be a married man, a man who has only one living wife."

Greene then asks, "How could these words be applied to single men?"[3]

J. Vernon McGee, who was one of my seminary professors, wrote about the unmarried pastor view and said, "It could mean that he ought to be married. I feel that Paul had this in mind."[4] Nevertheless, McGee, who was unmarried at the beginning of his pastoral ministry, admits that this must be a secondary meaning.[5]

This view raises several objections. First, Paul uses the numerical adjective "one," not the indefinite article "a." If Paul meant that a pastor had to be married, the phrase would have read, "a husband of a wife." Gromacki concludes that, "the addition of 'one' has significance."[6]

Another objection to this view is Paul himself. He was an elder, and he was not married. Arrington writes, "What about Paul? Was he married? The possibility cannot be categorically ruled out, but as far as we know, he was not. However, it is clear that he was an elder."[7] McGee argues that Paul had been married and was a widower. Nevertheless, this would still mean that he was unmarried at the time of his ministry.

If we maintain that a man is disqualified because he is not married, logically we also are forced to argue that he cannot be a pastor until he has at least two children. According to 1 Timothy 3:4, a bishop must have his *children*, not just his child, in subjection.

Jensen writes, "The requirement is not that a bishop must be married, but that if married he have no more than one wife at the time."[8] No doubt this is right in line with what the Apostle Paul meant. Kent adds an important note when he says, "The overseer must be the husband of 'one wife' not 'many.' Paul does not say he must be 'husband of a wife.'"[9]

In other words, Paul is not stating that a man must be married to be a pastor. Although I believe that a single man who is a pastor will face more challenges in the ministry. One challenge may be how to deal with all the dinner invitations from mothers of eligible young daughters!

2. Married to the Church

Roman Catholics teach that "The First Epistle to Timothy urges the bishop to be 'the husband of one wife'—interpreted as the Church."[10] Taylor says, "The Papists interpret it most ridiculously in an allegory, affirming that Paul's meaning is that an elder must have but one wife, and that must be his church."[11] Catholics spiritualize the phrase by saying that the life of the priest conforms to the chastity of Christ himself. The priest follows the example of Jesus Christ in being "married" to the Church.[12] This view puts much strain on the biblical text. Protestant interpreters reject this explanation.

An objection to this view is that Catholics do not allegorize the other qualities of the bishop found in 1 Timothy 3 and Titus 1. Most importantly, the mention of children in 1 Timothy 3:4 clearly indicates that this is not a spiritual marriage. Kent calls this "an obvious and rather clumsy attempt to protect the Romish doctrine of celibacy for priests."[13] In truth, this passage is one of the strongest proofs that the clergy may and usually should be married!

3. Loyalty to One-Wife

Getz[14] and Mounce,[15] hold this view that if married, a bishop must be loyal to his wife. However, it seems that Paul is saying more than simply that a bishop must be an example of strict morality. Of course, Paul was for marital fidelity, but this is obviously the duty of all believers, not simply of pastors. Furthermore, as Plummer argues, if Paul had this in mind, "He would have used much less ambiguous language than the phrase under discussion."[16]

4. Prohibition of Remarried Widowers

This view has had its share of followers. They hold that Paul's injunction disqualifies from the pastorate a man who remarries after his wife's death. In essence, those who uphold this teaching say that Paul forbids remarriage for a widowed pastor. Some Latin church fathers, such as Tertullian, held this view. Easton states, "The accepted explanation of this phrase in patristic Christianity was 'not a digamist,' i.e. 'not remarried after the death of a former wife.'"[17] This was a common belief in Europe and is the prevailing viewpoint in the Greek and Oriental churches.

Liddon argues for this interpretation and calls remarriage of a widower, "successive polygamy!"[18] Wuest, who prefers this view, states that an interpretative translation would be "married only once," and that this "gives the English reader in unmistakably clear language, the true meaning of the words in the A.V., 'the husband of one wife.'"[19]

Plummer spends seven pages arguing for this view. His four-fold defense is as follows: (1) Remarriage after the death of a spouse is a sign of weakness, and a bishop is supposed to be a man of strength. (2) A pastor must be above reproach. (3) Paul tells people to remain as they are. (4) Many early church fathers held this view.[20] To those who argue that a remarried widower may not be a pastor, J. P. Green responds, "It is really difficult to believe that they can be in earnest in their discussion of the question."[21]

The objections to this fourth view are: (1) While many of the early church fathers held this theory, some of them did not. For example, Theodore of Mopsuestia wrote, "Any man who lives on after the death of his first wife may legitimately take a second wife, as long as he lives in the same way with her as with the first [chastely], and ought not be prohibited from becoming a bishop."[22] Cyril of Jerusalem also permitted remarriage. He said, "Do not let the once-married set at nought those who have come together in marriage for the second time. For continence is a fine thing and admirable. But folk may be pardoned for contracting a second marriage."[23]

(2) It certainly is no more a sign of weakness for a widower to remarry than for a single man to marry. God instituted marriage and considered it holy. Moreover, the Bible says that marriage is honorable (Heb. 13:4), and that the one who finds a wife finds a good thing (Prov. 18:22). It is not sinful for a widower to remarry. Therefore, such a man is still above reproach.

(3) The apostle Paul did not tell everyone to remain as he was. Rather, he strongly encouraged young widows to remarry (1 Tim. 5:14).

(4) Remarriage after the death of a spouse is not successive polygamy. There is nothing sinful about remarrying after the death of a spouse. The Law of Moses required a man to marry a widowed sister-in-law and raise up children. The book of Ruth beautifully illustrates compliance to this levirate aspect of the Law.

"Nowhere does Scripture prohibit a second marriage after the death of the first spouse. Death cancels the marriage contract (Rom. 7:3), leaving the surviving partner free to marry again."[24]

5. Prohibition of Polygamy

This view has a special appeal in Western churches today because polygamy does not exist in most Western countries. Therefore, for those who hold this interpretation, the "husband of one wife" issue is of little consequence.

The advocates of this view argue that, since God instituted marriage as a monogamy, polygamy is sinful. Therefore, a polygamist is disqualified from the pastorate. This is certainly correct. Scripture forbids polygamy for all believers in 1 Corinthians 7:2.

However, did Paul have polygamy in mind when he penned the Pastoral Epistles? The answer is, "No." We must point out that, while polygamy was prevalent in Old Testament times, monogamy was the norm in the apostolic age. Roman law prohibited polygamy, and the Greeks considered it an infamous practice. "The prevailing type of marriage in Jewish, Greek, and Roman society was monogamous."[25]

The major objection to this viewpoint is that "No Christian, whether overseer or not, would ever have been allowed to practice polygamy."[26] Thus, Paul had no need to write against it. "Paul was certainly not referring to polygamy, since no church member, let alone a pastor, would be accepted if he had more than one wife."[27]

6. Prohibition of Divorce

The sixth view is that Paul was excluding from the pastorate any man who had been divorced. This interpretation of 1 Timothy 3:2 is the best one. "It fits a Jewish background, in the sense that a Jewish husband could very easily divorce his wife and remarry. A Jewish wife did not have such freedom, though in certain circumstances she could more or less compel her husband to divorce her. Similarly in Hellenistic society a husband could divorce his wife and remarry without difficulty. In Roman society divorce initiated by either spouse was notoriously easy."[28]

In Paul's day most of the members of the Gentile churches had come out of paganism with its low moral standards, including lax marriages. While any of these members could be genuinely saved and fully forgiven, only some qualified for the high office of the pastorate.

"Consequently, when men were to be considered for this high office, there must be no record of divorce or other marital infidelity in the candidate, even before his conversion. A very practical reason for this restriction is seen. Extremely embarrassing complications might occur in the church if the minister's divorced wife, mistresses, illegitimate children, or children of other marriages should come to light. Such a condition would at least lay him open to reproach, it would violate the general qualification of blamelessness."[29]

The Pastor and His Children

In 1 Timothy 3:4, Paul's directive is that a bishop must be "one who rules his own house well, having *his* children in subjection in all reverence." In Titus 1:6 we read that an elder must have "faithful children not accused of dissipation or insubordination." A pastor must run his household thoughtfully and have his children under control. The way a man manages his home reveals his capacity for leadership. Rebellious children would disqualify a man from the pastorate.

"The apostle lays heavy emphasis upon the pastor's care of his children. He must rear a respectable family, one which out of love acknowledges his authority. This pattern of love is absolutely essential because so much of the Christian gospel moves around the family relationships. If a pastor's family is disorderly, then the gospel he preaches is . . . set at naught by his example."[30]

No pastor is a perfect father, and neither are the pastor's children perfect. Just because a pastor's children misbehave on occasion, he is not disqualified. Every child, because of his or her sinful bent, will disobey at times. The issue is how the pastor and his wife deal with the child when this happens. Nevertheless, a man is disqualified if his children are disobedient most of the time, and a rebellious attitude is their way of life.

The question might arise, "What about a pastor who has four children and three of them serve the Lord, but one is rebellious?" In this case, we must remember that the pastor cannot force his children to serve the Lord. The three obedient children demonstrate that this pastor endeavored to lead the family in the right way. In the end, the rebellious child will have to answer to God. We may conclude from the other children that the pastor was a good father, and he would not be disqualified from serving in the pastoral office.

"However, if the majority of his children are yet unbelievers, he has certainly fallen short of this standard. Likewise, the general rule of thumb must be that his children are obedient and respectful. Certainly, there are times that even an elder's child will disobey and require discipline. This however should be the exception and not the rule. An elder must be a good parent, doing everything possible to be the spiritual leader of the family, providing direction, love, and discipline."[31] "The home life of the minister is his most potent instrument for good in the community."[32]

NOTES FOR
CHAPTER FIVE

[1] Kent, *Pastoral Epistles*, p. 124.

[2] Oliver B. Greene, *The Epistles*, p. 108.

[3] Ibid., 108.

[4] McGee, *I and II Timothy*, p.53.

[5] Ibid.

[6] Robert G. Gromacki, *Stand True to the Charge: An Exposition of I Timothy* (Grand Rapids: Baker Book House, 1982), p.80.

[7] French L. Arrington, *Maintaining the Foundations: A Study of I Timothy* (Grand Rapids: Baker Book House, 1982), p. 78.

[8] Irving L. Jensen, *1 & 2 Timothy and Titus: A Self-Study Guide* (Chicago: Moody Press, 1973), p. 38.

[9] Kent, *Pastoral Epistles,* p. 124.

[10] Wikipedia, Http://en.wikipedia.org/wiki/Clerical_celibacy, "Development of clerical celibacy in the Christian church," 2/21/2008.

[11] Thomas Taylor, *Exposition of Titus* (Minneapolis: Klock & Klock Christian Publishers, 1980), p. 88.

[12] Wikipedia, "Theological foundations," 2/21/2008.

[13] Kent, *Pastoral Epistles,* p. 122.

[14] Gene A. Getz, *A Profile for a Christian Life Style: A Study of Titus* (Grand Rapids: Zondervan Publishing House, 1978), p. 45.

[15] Mounce, *Pass It On,* p. 37.

[16] Alfred Plummer, *The Pastoral Epistles* (New York: George H. Doran, n. d.), p. 122.

[17] Burton Scott Easton, *The Pastoral Epistles* (New York: Charles Scribner's Sons), p. 212.

[18] H. P. Liddon, *Explanatory Analysis of St. Paul's First Epistle to Timothy* (Minneapolis: Klock & Klock Christian Publishers, 1978), p. 26.

[19] Kenneth S. Wuest, *The Pastoral Epistles in the Greek New Testament for the English Reader* (Grand Rapids: Wm. B. Eerdmans Publishing Co., 1952), p. 54-55.

[20] Plummer, *Pastoral Epistles*, pp. 122-129.

[21] J. P. Greene, *The Pastoral Epistles: 1st and 2nd Timothy, Titus* in *The Convention Series* (Nashville: Sunday School Board, Southern Baptist Convention, 1915), pp. 45-46.

[22] Theodore of Mopsuestia on "1 Timothy 3:2b" in *Ancient Christian Commentary on Scripture: New Testament IX: Colossians, 1-2 Thessalonians, 1-2 Timothy, Titus, Philemon*, edited by Peter Gorday (Downers Grove, IL: InterVarsity Press, 2000), p. 170.

[23] Cyril of Jerusalem on "1 Timothy 3:2b" in *Ancient Christian Commentary on Scripture*, p. 170.

[24] Arrington, *Maintaining*, p. 79.

[25] Everett Ferguson, *Backgrounds of Early Christianity* (Grand Rapids: Willaim B. Eerdmans Publishing Company, 1993), p. 69.

[26] Guthrie, *The Pastoral Epistles*, p. 80.

[27] Wiersbe, *Be Faithful*, p. 42.

[28] Hanson, *The Pastoral*, p. 78.

[29] Kent, *Pastoral Epistles*, p. 125.

[30] Trentham, *Studies*, p. 41.

[31] Gary L Hauck, *Consistent Living: Titus & Philemon* (Schaumburg, IL: Regular Baptist Press, 1997), p.16.

[32] Harold L. Longenecker, *Building Town & Country Churches* (Chicago: Moody Press, 1973), p. 102.

Chapter 6

THE PASTOR AND OTHERS

As a husband and father, a pastor's relationship to his wife and children is fundamental. Moreover, by virtue of his position as a pastor and as a citizen, his relationship to his church and his world are also important. Paul gives several qualifications of a pastor that relate to his ministry in the church and in the world.

The Pastor and His Church

A Hospitable Host

Philoxenon (1 Tim. 3:2; Tit. 1:8). This term appears in both passages concerning the pastor, and it is translated "hospitable" in each case. It literally means "a lover of strangers." This hospitality ministry was important, especially in that day when inns were often dangerous and were places of ill repute. "Christians when travelling were reluctant to use public inns—for moral as well as ceremonial reasons—and depended on members of their own religion for entertainment. So 'caring for strangers' was an imperative religious duty."[1]

As persecution against Christianity increased in the early church, hospitality became a ministry that benefited Christians who became homeless because of persecution. The pastor's home was a refuge for servants of the Lord. A pastor who was a hospitable host also welcomed preachers and teachers who traveled from church to church.

Likewise today, "a Christian leader must be hospitable, generous to guests—with an open home and an open heart. He does not view guests as interruptions to his personal agenda, but as opportunities to share the love and blessing of the Lord."[2]

A Skilled Teacher

Didaktikon (1 Tim. 3:2). This "adjective does not mean 'teachable,' but 'apt at teaching.'"[3] Paul told the Ephesians that Christ had given the church gifted men to equip the saints for the ministry. Among these gifted men Paul listed pastors and teachers (Eph. 4:11).

A pastor has the dual responsibility of caring for his flock and teaching. "He must have both the understanding of biblical truth and the necessary oral and verbal skills to communicate that truth."[4] The Holy Spirit enables the pastor to carry out this ministry by sovereignly bestowing upon him the gift of teaching (Rom. 12:7; 1 Cor. 12:28-29). While teaching is a gift, this does not excuse the pastor from long hours of diligent study and training in the Scriptures. "The pastor who is lazy in his study is a disgrace in the pulpit."[5]

The Pastor and His World

A pastor is also a man who must relate to his world, but he must not be conformed to worldly thinking and practices (Rom. 12:2). His conduct should be a living testimony to the gospel he proclaims. Paul described two qualities required of the pastor concerning his relationship with those outside the church.

A Lover of Good

Philagathon (Tit. 1:8). The KJV translates this term, "a lover of good men." The NKJV renders it "a lover of what is good." Literally it is simply "a lover of good," which includes both people and things. A pastor should be a man who is devoted to all that is beneficial, and he should be an ally of everything that is worthwhile. On the one hand, a pastor should never neglect his study time. On the other hand, he should take a break from his studies periodically and participate in some activities even though they are not religious.

A pastor may enjoy good music, art, and literature. He may volunteer in philanthropic community endeavors and in health organizations like the heart or lung association. He may even be involved in civic events without compromising his stand. My older son, who is my current pastor, preaches at the city's memorial services. He agreed to do so on a rotating basis. Consequently when his turn comes up, he is the only pastor there; and he has the freedom to preach the gospel clearly.

A Man of Good Reputation in the Community

Martyrian kalen echein apo ton exothen (1 Tim. 3:7). The literal meaning and word order of this phrase is "a good testimony to have from the ones outside." The pastor must have a good reputation in the community, not just in the church. "Those who are outside" definitely refers to those who are outside of the church. It is from this group that the pastor is to win new converts, so he must be of good report among them. It is the unsaved people of the community who are giving the testimony this time, and they testify as to the pastor's character. "What a candidate says about himself, what the church sees, and what the unsaved report should all agree."[6]

Paul offers two reasons why a pastor should have a good reputation. One reason is so that he may not fall into justifiable criticism by the unsaved. It is possible that they may be aware of something about which the church has no information.

Another reason is so that he will not fall into some trap laid by the devil that would ruin his ministry. Satan desires nothing more than to snare a pastor and bring his church into disrepute. Upright living by the pastor in his community will do much to prevent the success of such a plot. A pastor must select his affiliations carefully and not compromise in his stand in the community. At the same time, he must be a blessing and an example to all about him.

God's call to a man to serve in the pastorate is truly a high calling. "No man has a right to go into the ministry without sufficient assurance that it is the will of God."[7] Likewise, no man has a right to go into the pastorate without meeting the biblical qualifications required by the Apostle Paul in 1 Timothy 3 and Titus 1.

The apostle sets forth a high standard for the pastoral office. This is not surprising because this is the highest office in the local church, and the local church is the center of God's program for this age. In his purpose for writing to Timothy, Paul calls the church "the house of God, which is the church of the living God, the pillar and ground of the truth" (1 Tim. 3:15). All of us in the ministry must faithfully review 1 Timothy 3 and Titus 1, and we must live in obedience to God's requirements delineated in these chapters.

NOTES FOR CHAPTER SIX

[1] Hauck, *Consistent Living*, p. 16.

[2] Ibid. p. 18.

[3] Kent, *Pastoral Epistles*, p. 127.

[4] Gromacki, *Stand True*, p. 82.

[5] Wiersbe, *Be Faithful*, p. 43.

[6] Gromacki, *Stand True*, p. 86.

[7] Mark W. Lee, *The Minister and His Ministry* (Grand Rapids: Zondervan Publishing House, 1960), p. 13.

Chapter 7

THE PASTOR'S REWARD

A faithful pastor may receive many rewards such as the love of the people who make up his flock, the joy of seeing believers grow in the grace and knowledge of Jesus Christ, and the fellowship with the saints in his congregation. All these are great rewards, but the ultimate reward is even more precious: a crown of glory!

In writing to pastors, the apostle Peter states, "When the Chief Shepherd appears, you will receive the crown of glory that does not fade away" (1 Peter 5:4). The Chief Shepherd, Jesus Christ, will award this crown at the Bema seat, which takes place right after the Rapture of the church.

The Scriptures mention other crowns: The crown of rejoicing for bringing people to Christ (1 Thess. 2:19); the crown of righteousness for loving the coming of Christ (2 Tim. 4:8); the incorruptible crown for living a disciplined life for the sake of the gospel (I Cor. 9:25); and the crown of life for enduring testing and for being faithful until death (James 1:12; Rev. 2:10). Christ will award these crowns to faithful believers in general. However, the crown of glory is specifically for pastors who are faithful to their responsibilities in the church.

The crown of glory mentioned by Peter (*tes doxes stephanon*) "is a sign of special honour, given not to all but only as a reward for some kind of unusually meritorious activity. Such an idea would fit this verse, where Peter mentions this unfading crown of glory specifically when speaking to 'elders.'"[1] Barton describes this crown within the context of the culture in the Greco-Roman world: "The 'crown' while metaphorical, pictures the laurel-wreath crown that was given to winners in the Greek and Roman athletic games. A symbol of triumph and honor, this was the most coveted prize of ancient times."[2] Faithful pastors also will receive a reward of triumph and honor, only theirs will not fade away. Earthly laurel-wreath crowns eventually faded, dried up, and disintegrated, but the crown of glory that faithful pastors will receive is unchanging and eternal.

This crown belongs to a glorious celestial realm. "At the second coming, when all Christians are summed before the judgment seat of Christ (2 Cor. 5:10), the elders who have been true to their commission will receive the crown of glory that can never be subject to the ravages of time, for it belongs to another world-order."[3] Scripture does not reveal what the crown of glory will be like, because human language is not adequate to describe spiritual, heavenly realities.

McNight believes that it is not wise to think of this as a physical crown, but rather as "the crown of glory of being accepted by God."[4] Hillyer claims that the grammar of the expression, "crown of glory," allows for several explanations: (1) a crown which is in some way composed of glory (1 Pet 4:14); (2) a glorious crown that will never lose its dazzling brightness; (3) a crown symbolizing a share in the divine glory (2 Pet. 1:4);

and (4) if a royal crown is in mind, it may hint to greater responsibilities in the world to come (Matt. 19:18; 25:21, cf. 1 Pet. 2:9.)[5]

The Chief Shepherd will recompense abundantly each faithful pastor. "The elder will receive [a] reward far beyond the value of any earthly remuneration."[6] The Pastor's reward will not be in terms of this earthly world, but in a form appropriate to his everlasting life in heaven with God. Is it possible that the crown of glory involves a special capacity to reflect Christ's glory in heaven? A positive answer to this question may explain why the glory of this crown does not fade away.

In this earth only pastor/shepherds can truly reflect the image of the Chief Shepherd, as they lovingly lead and feed His sheep (cf. 1 Pet. 5:2-4 with John 10:1-30, and John 21:15-17). Accordingly in heaven it will be the privilege of pastors to reflect this glorious shepherding aspect of Christ's image! What greater motivation for selfless service could there be than this!

Only the Chief Shepherd knows the essential character of the crown of glory, but "whatever the nature of that crown, it is clearly intended as a symbol of triumph and represents a sharing in the victory of Jesus Christ over all suffering and over death itself (1 Pet. 5:1)."[7]

Hiebert reminds his readers that the difficulties of the pastors' work, "as well as their consciousness of their own inadequacies and failures, would often discourage the most prudent."[8] However, Calvin provides the antidote to potential discouragement in the pastoral ministry because of trials: "To prevent the faithful servant of Christ from being cast down, there is this one and only remedy, to turn his eyes to the coming of Christ."[9] Then each faithful pastor will receive his heavenly reward!

NOTES FOR
CHAPTER SEVEN

[1] Wayne Grudem, *1 Peter* in *The Tyndale New Testament Commentaries* (Grand Rapids: William B. Eerdman Publishing Company, 1988), pp. 190-191.

[2] Bruce B. Barton, Mark Fackler, Linda K. Taylor, and Dave Veerman, *1 and 2 Peter, Jude* in *Life Application Bible Commentary* (Wheaton IL: Tyndale House Publishers, Inc., 1995), p. 133.

[3] Norman Hillyer, *1 and 2 Peter, Jude* in the *New International Biblical Commentary* (Peabody, MA: Hendrickson Publishers, 1992), p. 141.

[4] Scot McKnight, *1 Peter* in *The NIV Application Commentary*, (Grand Rapids: Zondervan, 1996), p. 263.

[5] Hillyer, *1 and 2 Peter*, p. 141.

[6] Ibid., p. 140.

[7] Ibid., p. 141.

[8] D. Edmond Hiebert, *1 Peter* (Winona Lake, IN: BMH Books, 1992), p. 306.

[9] John Calvin, *The Epistle of Paul the Apostle to the Hebrews and the First and Second Epistles of St. Peter* in *Calvin's Commentaries* (Grand Rapids: William B. Eerdmans Publishing Company, 1963), p. 317.

Part Two

The Office of Deacons

Chapter 8

WERE "THE SEVEN" DEACONS OR NOT?

Commentators disagree on the origin of deacons as an office in the apostolic church. The debate involves the role of "the seven" in Acts 6, where we find that the infant church was growing rapidly. The apostles could not adequately keep up with the work of ministering to such a large group of people. Acts 6:1 describes the specific problem: "Now in those days, when *the number of* disciples was multiplying, there arose a complaint against the Hebrews by the Hellenists, because their widows were neglected in the daily distribution."

The Hellenists (Grecians in the KJV) were Greek-speaking Jews, while the Hebrews were Aramaic-speaking Jews. The mother tongue of the apostles was Aramaic. Naturally the apostles heard the needs of the Aramaic widows more readily, while they neglected the Greek-speaking widows. This was causing contention in the church, so the apostles told the members to choose seven qualified men to help them: "Then the twelve summoned the multitude of the disciples and said, 'It is not desirable that we should leave the word of God and serve tables'" (Acts 6:2). Serving tables involved the distribution of food items or money for needy widows.

According to verse 5, the words of the apostles pleased the congregation, and they chose seven men. The role of these men is a debatable issue. The question is whether they were simply helpers, pre-deacons, or men who actually held the office of deacons. Agar in his book, *The Deacons at Work*, is an example of those who see no connection between Acts 6 and the origin of the deacons. He writes, "A careful reading of Acts 6:1-8 would seem to give no basis for the general belief that therein is found an account of the first election of deacons."[1] However, many do go back to Acts 6 for the beginning of the office of deacon, some rather cautiously, and others with more certainty.

One view is that the seven were temporary helpers. Advocates of this view base it on two reasons: "First, these men were chosen for a particular task, not an overall one. Second, they were in a temporary responsibility because of the communal nature of the church in Jerusalem."[2]

Johnson acknowledges, "Although the title *diakonoi* is not given them by Luke, the seven appointed by the church to oversee the distribution to the Gentile widows in Acts 6:1-6 clearly fit into this category of helper."[3]

Another view is that the seven were forerunners of deacons, or pre-deacons, and that their position eventually evolved into the office of deacon as we know it today. Guthrie seems to refer to the seven chosen men of Acts 6 as some kind of pre-deacons. He writes, "The earliest allusion to a class of people especially appointed for practical work is found in Acts 6, although the word 'deacon' is not there used."[4] Even some, who hold that they were not the first deacons, concede that "these men do illustrate the role and function of the office of deacons."[5]

The third view is that the seven were in fact the first deacons of the Jerusalem church. Kent argues that Acts 6 describes the origin of deacons. He says, "It seems almost certain to me that the title of the office, and probably the office itself, was derived from the choosing of the seven in Acts 6."[6] Jackson agrees that these men are the first deacons and says this about them: "Almost certainly they first appear in Scripture in Acts 6:1-8. They are to be godly men, filled with the Holy Spirit."[7]

Fremont, strongly argues that the book of Acts speaks of the deacons' office: "Acts 6:1-8:40 tells of the urgent need the church had for the office and work of deacons, and of the qualifications, call and work of these first deacons in the Jerusalem church."[8] Similarly, Cobb unquestionably affirms, "We learn from Acts 6 of the origin of the deaconship in the church."[9]

Personally, I agree with those who hold that the office of deacons originated in Jerusalem during the time period of Acts 6. We find in this chapter not only the "birth" of deacons in the context of a growing infant Church, but we also learn about their role and their qualifications.

NOTES FOR
CHAPTER EIGHT

[1] Frederick A. Agar, *The Deacon at Work* (Chicago: The Judson Press, 1923), p. 9.

[2] Stanley D. Toussaint, "Acts" in *The Bible Knowledge Commentary, New Testament Edition,* Edited by John F. Walvoord and Roy B. Zuck (Wheaton, IL: Victor Books, 1983), p. 368.

[3] Luke Timothy Johnson, *Letters to Paul's Delegates, 1 Timothy, 2 Timothy, Titus: The New Testament in Context* (Valley Forge, PA: Trinity Press International, 1996), p. 153.

[4] Guthrie, *The Pastoral Epistles*, p. 95.

[5] Toussaint, "Acts," p. 368.

[6] Kent, *Pastoral Epistles*, p. 132.

[7] Jackson, *Doctrine and Administration*, p. 42.

[8] Carson K. Fremont, *The Qualifications, Training and Use of New Testament Deacons* (no place, no publisher, no date), p. 3.

[9] J. E. Cobb, *Cobb's Baptist Church Manual*, rev. ed. (Little Rock, AR: Baptist Publications Committee of the Baptist Missionary Association of America, 1972), p. 72.

Chapter 9

INTRODUCTION TO THE OFFICE OF DEACONS

In the last chapter we studied "the seven" and concluded that Acts 6 gives us the origin of the office of deacons. Several important questions remain. What function did they fulfill in the early church? What is their function today? How long should they serve? How do they relate to the overseers? These questions need answers. We will strive to answer some of them in this chapter and will examine others in later chapters. For the answers to these questions, we will turn to the Bible and begin with a study of the word *diakonos*.

The Word *Diakonos*

Our English word "deacon" is not a translation but rather a transliteration of the Greek word *diakonos*. "The term 'deacon' refers literally to someone who serves."[1] According to the New Testament usage, *diakonos* can refer to diverse positions and types of service.

Campbell lists the different people to whom Paul applied the term *diakonos*: to a civil ruler (Rom. 13:4); to Christ as a minister (*diakonon*) to the Jews (Rom. 15:8); to Phoebe as a servant (*diakonon*) of the church in Chenchrea (Rom. 16:1); to himself and Apollos as ministers (*diakonoi*) through whom the Corinthians believed (1 Cor. 3:5); to himself as a qualified minister (*diakonous*) of the new covenant (2 Cor. 3:6) and a minister (*diakonos*) of the Gospel (Eph. 3:7); and to Thychicus as a faithful minister (*diakonos*) in the Lord (Eph. 6:21).[2]

Sometimes the New Testament uses *diakonos* as a general term to refer to a person who functions as a servant or as a helper of some kind (Matt. 20:26). At other times *diakonos* refers to a position, such as in Philippians 1:1, where the KJV and NKJV rightly translate the plural form as "deacons." Some modern versions use different terms to translate the word *diakonos*. For example, the *New Living Translation* renders it "authorities" in Romans 13:4.

Fee summarizes this double meaning of the term: "The word seems to fluctuate between an emphasis on a *function* and a description of a *position*; by the time of Philippians it describes an 'office' (Phil. 1:1)"[3] (italics in original). Nonetheless, even when the term refers to the office of deacon, the deaconship involves the idea of service. "Men are to be elected to the office of deacon with a view to service."[4]

The Term "Deacon Board"

Is the term "Deacon Board" biblical? The answer is "No!" The New Testament designation for a group of men serving in the diaconate office is *deacons* (1 Tim. 3). The title *Deacon Board* is non-existent in Scripture.

The phrase "board of deacons" crept into Baptist churches from other groups. "Evidences are abundant that the denominations which maintain a central ruling authority have directly influenced the Baptist people. *The drift among Baptists may be clearly traced*—it is seen in the adoption and use of the word 'board' as applied to the deacons so that this company becomes a *board of deacons*"[5] (Italics in original).

In 1846 Dr. Howell, pastor of the First Baptist Church in Nashville, Tennessee, first applied the term "board" in reference to deacons of a Baptist church.[6] As the use of this term spread, John Broadus vigorously spoke out against this "newly-coined phrase." (Broadus was a leading nineteenth-century Southern Baptist pastor, scholar, and later president of the Southern Baptist Seminary in Louisville, Kentucky.) However, "the protests and warnings of Dr. Broadus and others with him were of little avail."[7]

Burroughs perceptively describes the outcome of disregarding the warnings of these men: "That the concern which those men felt was not altogether without foundation is evident in the fact that now in some instances the deacons direct and guide the affairs of the church quite as fully as any board of directors controls the bank or the school."[8]

The confusion caused by the use of the term *board* has continued to plague many churches. Roger McNamara, in his excellent book on church planting, states that the word *board* "is a misnomer that creates an unbiblical concept. It leads deacons (and others) to believe they are an executive board that makes decisions and tells people what to do. That is not scriptural."[9]

Jackson concurs, "Unfortunately, some deacon 'boards' conceive of themselves to be a board of directors in charge of the corporation, and feel that under their direction the pastor, and even the people, must move in full obedience. Nothing could be farther from the New Testament position."[10]

The biblical role of deacons is not to rule the affairs of the church. "Their duties are indicated by their name, 'servants,' and by their relationship to the pastor as described in 1 Timothy 3—the second officers or assistants to the pastor."[11]

As I mentioned in the author's preface, I have been a deacon in several Baptist churches and currently serve as one at Faith Baptist Church in Cambridge, Iowa. Clearly I am not against the office of deacons. However, I have to agree that the term "board" *can* lead to a non-biblical perception of what the office of deacons is and what role this office entails.

Our church constitution at Maranatha had the term "board" in reference to the deacons. When we applied to join the Iowa Association of Regular Baptist Churches, one of the council members strongly advised us to remove this term from our constitution. We took his advice and removed it by church vote in a business meeting.

What terms should we use to refer to the deacons? "Servant leaders" is closer to the biblical term, while "fellowship of deacons" stresses companionship in a common cause with each other and the pastor. Most importantly, the latter designation points to their communion with each other and with Jesus Christ.

NOTES FOR
CHAPTER NINE

[1] Thomas D. Lea, and Hay P. Griffin, Jr., *1, 2 Timothy, Titus* in *The New American Commentary* (Nashville: Broadman Press, 1992), p.115.

[2] Earnest R. Campbell, *A Commentary of First Timothy* (Silverton, OR: Canyonview Press, 1983), p.112.

[3] Gordon D. Fee, *1 and 2 Timothy, Titus* in the *New International Biblical Commentry* (Peabody, MA: Hendrickson Publishers, Inc., 1995), p. 86.

[4] P. E. Burroughs, *Honoring the Deaconship*, rev. ed. (Nashville: The Sunday School Board of the Southern Baptist Convention, 1936), p. 12.

[5] Ibid., p. 16.

[6] Roger McNamara and Ken Davis, *The YBH Handbook of Church Planting* (no place: Xulon Press, Baptist Mid-Missions, 2005), p. 488.

[7] Burroughs, *Honoring the Deaconship*, p.16.

[8] Ibid., p. 17.

[9] McNamara, *YBH*, p. 488.

[10] Jackson, *Doctrine & Administration*, p. 42.

[11] Ibid., p. 51.

Chapter 10

THE CHOSEN FEW OF ACTS 6

Introduction

"It is honorable to be a deacon."[1]

The Bible lists the God-ordained qualifications for pastors, and it also gives the qualifications God requires of the deacons. As we saw in chapter 9 of this study, the biblical passages containing these traits are Acts 6 and 1 Timothy 3. We will begin with Acts 6, where we find the qualities that the Jerusalem congregation had to consider in selecting those first deacons whom the apostles then appointed. The apostles laid down three of these qualities, and Luke noted an additional one, which was a trait of Stephen, and should be of all deacons in order to be filled by the Spirit.

A Good Reputation

The first qualification is a rendering of the word *Marturoumenous* (Acts 6:3). The apostles addressed the early church with these words, "Therefore, brethren, seek out from among you seven men of good reputation." In the active voice the Greek verb *martureo* means "to be a witness, to bear testimony to something." In the passive it has the idea of "being well reported of, accredited, and approved." Thus, *marturoumenous* "has two uses—it can mean a person of whom a good witness is given and also a person who is good in witnessing."[2]

These seven chosen deacons, who were to be special helpers to the apostles, were men whose lives bore witness to the life changing gospel by deed as well as by word. "Certainly the apostles wanted people of impeccable character, but that character should be a witness to Christ in them and activate involvement in communicating His love to others.[3] For this church office, "the virtues of . . . truthfulness, . . . and rigid honesty were indispensable."[4]

Filled with the Spirit

This qualification is a translation of *plereis pneumatos* (Acts 6:3), "Full of the Spirit." This filling of the Spirit "was to be exemplified in all dimensions of their lives—intellectual, emotional, volitional."[5]

The filling of the Spirit means allowing Him to control our lives. This requires our obedience to God's Word, resulting in the Spirit's transforming us into the image of Christ (cf. Eph. 5:18; Gal. 5:16, 22-23). In the case of obedient deacons, when they are filled with the Spirit, He transforms them into servants like their Lord Jesus Christ who "did not come to be served, but to serve and to give His life a ransom for many" (Mark 10:45, see also Phil. 2:1-8). Christ-like service in the church requires Spirit-filling!

Full of Wisdom

Plereis . . . sophias (Acts 6:3). "In Acts 6:3 when the disciples spoke of having wisdom, it was a matter of having godly understanding—godly understanding from God and for Him. An individual can be ever so good and prudent, but if he is void of understanding, his profit is very limited. One cannot succeed without the wisdom of God."[6] A connection exists between the filling of the Holy Spirit and wisdom: Ogilvie calls wisdom the test of Spirit filling in a deacon, and he also says that "The evidence of the Spirit's indwelling would be the gift to penetrate the deep mysteries of God and apply them in guidance for daily life."[7]

The Bible states that the fear of the Lord is the beginning of both knowledge and wisdom (Ps. 111:10; Prov. 1:7). True wisdom requires knowledge of God and reverence for Him, evidenced by obedience to His Word. Godly wisdom is the product of Christ-like responses to everyday life experiences. This means living by our knowledge of God's Word. Deacons must possess this godly wisdom. The diversity of their ministries to the congregation and to its leader requires wisdom. A pastor benefits greatly from the advice of deacons who are full of godly wisdom.

Full of Faith

Pleres pisteos. (Acts 6:5). In his description of Stephen, one of the first seven deacons, Luke notes that he was a man "full of faith" and "of the Holy Spirit." Just one chapter later in Acts 7, Stephen faced martyrdom. He was a godly deacon who lived and died by faith. His faith in God sustained him as he witnessed even to the point of death! Stephen, who was "full of faith and of the Holy Spirit," was at the top of the list of these early servants of the church. Today's deacons also should be strong in the faith.

In the fall of 1995, God granted me the opportunity to serve Him with deacons who were full of faith. That year the Lord led my wife and me to plant a new church in a suburb of Des Moines, Iowa. We started with the two of us and $75.00. God blessed, and the work grew. After a year and four months, we had about forty-five members and $30,000 in our building fund.

At the beginning of 1997, as the deacons and I met to set up the budget for the new year, I asked them what amount should be our goal at the year's end for the building fund. They said, "$100,000!" Since we only had forty-five members, including some older children, I thought that this amount was extremely high. However, I did not want to dampen the deacons' faith. So I said, "That is a lot! We will have to have faith and pray every day that God will enable us to reach that goal."

Instead of the usual thermometer, I sketched a scene of a little country church on a poster to encourage us to give. The church was surrounded by trees, bushes, and sky. Then I drew lines over the picture dividing it into 100 squares, each representing $1,000. Since we had $30,000 on hand already, I colored in thirty squares at random. Each time $1,000 more came in, I colored in another square, which could be a piece of sky, the door, a window, a bush, or part of a tree. The congregation watched excitedly as more and more of the picture began to show up in color. We prayed, and gave, and trusted God. He provided the money and allowed us the joy of coloring square after square of the church poster.

That year, December 31 landed on a Sunday. When the deacons finished counting the evening offering, the building fund stood at $100,061.18! God was faithful to answer our prayers. To Him be the glory! I praise God for the faith of those early deacons!

NOTES FOR CHAPTER TEN

[1] Oliver B. Greene, *The Epistles*, p. 122.

[2] Lloyd J. Ogilvie, *Acts* in *The Communicator's Commentary:* (Waco, TX: Word Books, Publisher, 1983), p. 136.

[3] Ibid.

[4] Easton, *The Pastoral Epistles*, p. 132.

[5] Ogilvie, *Acts*, p. 136.

[6] C. P. Briley, *The Deacon's Life and His Wife* (Chapel Hill, NC: no publisher, 1962), p. 12.

[7] Ogilvie, *Acts*, p. 136.

Chapter 11

WHAT A DEACON SHOULD NOT BE

Introduction

While some may argue that "the seven" of Acts 6 were not the first deacons, no one argues that 1 Timothy 3:8-13 delineates the requirements for the office of deacons. Though "in the New Testament the word (*diakonos*) appears very seldom in a technical sense,"[1] its technical sense in this passage is undeniable.

The regulations for the office of deacons closely parallel those for the pastor (bishop). The context makes this clear by the use of the word "likewise" (3:8). "Neither office can be simply taken up without an inquiry into character."[2] As with the pastor, let us investigate the negative requirements first.

Not Double Tongued

Me dilogous (1 Timothy 3:8). The word, *dilogous* carries the idea of saying the same thing twice, repeating, double tongued, double in speech, saying one thing to one person and a different thing to another.

This is what Hoste says about a double tongued man: "It is the failing of the man of weak character who tries at all costs to escape disagreeing with any one. He finds a form of words suitable to each case, and both sides in a controversy think he backs them. Such a man rapidly loses moral weight."[3]

In contrast, a deacon "must not be guilty of saying one thing and meaning another. He must be a man of straight-forward, honest dealing; a man of clear, decisive speech. He must be a man who means what he says, in whom the people have confidence."[4] If he makes a promise, he must keep it.

Kent explains the importance of not selecting double tongued deacons. He writes, "Persons who spread conflicting tales among the congregation are not to be selected as deacons. Since the ministrations of such an officer would conceivably take him on constant rounds of visitation, a double tongued person would spread havoc in short order. This officer must know how to bridle his tongue."[5]

Not Given to Much Wine

Me oino pollo prosechontas (1 Timothy 3:8). *Oinos* is "wine." *Pollo* is "much or many" (as in polygamy); *prosechontas* means "to turn around, to turn to, to bring near, to be given to, to resign to, to be addicted to." The *me* meaning "not" makes it negative. A deacon is a man who is "not given to much wine" (KJV and NKJV).

"Many brethren have taken a great deal of comfort from the fact that while the preacher is not to use wine, the deacon is simply not to use *much* wine."[6] However, "When Paul made the statement 'not given to much wine,' he did not leave a loophole for deacons to drink, so long as they do not become drunken. They are not to yield to the temptation of strong drink."[7]

"There is no real ground for believing that a double standard is created by the Scriptures. A deacon has a responsibility towards God in the matter of alcoholic drink"[8] In fact, "The two further comments forbidding wine addicts and men of insatiable appetites for dishonest gain are both expressed in stronger terms than in the case of the overseers."[9]

Nichols points out that "in the time of Jesus and Paul, wine was used as a substitute for water because of the scarcity and lack of purity of water. In all of recorded history there have been some who have overindulged in strong drink and the warning here is against such a practice by a deacon. If Paul were living today, in view of the fact that water is plenteous and pure, he would probably say; 'not given to drinking intoxicating beverages.'"[10]

Kent concurs when he says, "The fact that deacons were not told to become total abstainers but rather to be temperate, does not mean that Christians today can use liquor in moderate amounts."[11] Kent then makes the following observations concerning this issue: (1) In Paul's day, the wine used as a common beverage was mostly water. (2) The social stigma and social evils that accompany drinking today did not come with the wine that people drank in their homes back then. (3) Paul's principle that believers should not do anything to

"This job gets better by the week!"

cause a brother to stumble in time came to be applied to the use of wine.[12]

Kent closes his discussion on wine and deacons with this exhortation "Certainly in present-day America, the use of wine by a Christian would abet a recognized social evil, and would set a most dangerous example for the young and the weak. To us Paul would undoubtedly say, 'No wine at all.'"[13]

Not Greedy for Money

Me aischrokerdeis (I Tim. 3:8). *Aischrokerdeis* comes from *aischros*, which means "dishonorable, base" and from *kerdos* "gain, advantage." The KJV renders *aischrokerdeis* as "not greedy of filthy lucre." The phrase contains a compound adjective that refers to money. It means "fond of sordid gain" (NASB). "This is a person who is above wanting to make money under any circumstances, fair or foul."[14]

"It seems most natural to refer it [greedy of base gains] to dishonesty with the alms of the Church or any abuse of their spiritual office for purposes of gain."[15] A deacon often faced the temptation to succumb to greediness since he dispersed money as well as food to the poor. "The office of deacon gave the holder opportunity to yield to this impulse. If his work involved the distribution of alms to the needy, there was a chance for embezzlement. Anyone who has access to church finances has opportunity to act dishonestly."[16]

As I mentioned in an earlier chapter (p. 36), no one should ever count the offering alone, and it is never wise to ask a deacon to do so. He may be perfectly honest, but this leaves him open to accusations of embezzlement. Under these circumstances no eye witness is present to defend him from such accusations. In my years of ministry as a pastor, I never counted the offering, nor did I ever ask a deacon to count it alone. Moreover, as a deacon I never counted alone. If for some reason, no other deacon was present, I asked another mature, faithful man to help me.

The world delights to see a pastor or deacon fall to temptation in the area of church finances. "No one will feel surprised at the emphasis laid on this matter when he recollects with what sharp eyes the public looks for signs of self-interest in those who profess to be Bible believing Christians."[17] Regretfully, not all deacons have been above board in financial matters. Some have helped themselves to church funds and have brought disgrace to the cause of Christ. Financial gain should not be the motivating factor in ministry, but rather a desire to serve God.

NOTES FOR
CHAPTER ELEVEN

[1] C. K. Barrett, *The Pastoral Epistles* in the *New English Bible* (Oxford: Clarendon Press, 1963), p. 60.

[2] Ibid.

[3] William Hoste, *Bishops, Priests, and Deacons* (Kilmarnock, Great Britain: John Ritchie Publishers, no date), p. 132.

[4] Oliver B. Greene, *The Epistles*, p. 124.

[5] Kent, *Pastoral Epistles*, p. 132.

[6] Robert E. Naylor, *The Baptist Deacon* (Nashville: Broadman Press, 1955), p. 23.

[7] Oliver B. Greene, *The Epistles*, pp. 124-25.

[8] Naylor, *Baptist Deacon*, p. 23.

[9] Guthrie, *The Pastoral Epistles*, p. 95.

[10] Harold Nichols, *The Work of the Deacon and Deaconess* (Valley Forge PA: The Judson Press, 1964), pp. 8-9.

[11] Kent, *Pastoral Epistles*, p. 133.

[12] Ibid.

[13] Ibid.

[14] Manford George Gutzke, *Plain Talk on Timothy, Titus, and Philemon* (Grand Rapids: Zondervan, 1978), p. 52.

[15] C. J. Ellicott, *A Critical and Grammatical Commentary on the Pastoral Epistles* (London: Parker, Son, and Bourn, West Strand, 1861), p. 46.

[16] Kent, *Pastoral Epistles*, p. 134.

[17] J. Oswald Dykes, *The Christian Minister and His Duties* (Edinburgh: T. & T. Clark, 1909), p. 56.

Chapter 12

WHAT A DEACON SHOULD BE

Like the pastor, the deacons must live according to their new life in Christ. They must put off ungodly traits and put on Christ-like characteristics. In 1 Timothy 3 Paul sets forth the positive qualities that these church officers should evidence in their lives. We now turn to these godly traits.

Grave/Reverent

Semnous (1 Tim. 3:8). This word means "grave, august, venerable, honorable, to be venerated for character." "When the word 'grave' is used, the idea is brought out that he [a deacon] is to be serious-minded, not shifty, but reliable, responsible, good."[1] This word is also found in Titus 2:2, where Paul uses it of older Christian men in general. When used of a person, as here in the Pastoral Epistles, the term means "that a person is 'worthy of respect.'"[2]

Semnous is a positive term, and so in reference to deacons, "It denotes a seriousness of mind and character. Their service will be done in the name of the whole congregation, and thus is not to be lightly undertaken. (The word does not mean austere or unbending, however.)"[3]

A deacon must be serious minded or honorable, not silly or nonsensical. He must not have the reputation of being a clown. My wife's family had a friend who always was joking. He did not have a serious bone in his body. His string of funny stories attracted people to him, and his boisterous and frivolous behavior made him the focus of any gathering.

In reality he loved to be the center of attention. One day at home he shouted to his wife and children, "Quick! Take me to the doctor! I'm having a heart attack!" They all laughed. He said, "I'm serious!" He never was serious. So they really laughed. Right then he dropped dead of a heart attack!

In contrast, a deacon should be balanced and consign fun to its proper place. Appropriate seriousness will not quench a happy spirit. For example, serious discussions take place in pastor and deacons' meetings, but when harmony exists between the pastor and deacons, these meetings can be enjoyable and may be sprinkled with humor, within reason.

Fee provides this important fact about *semnous*: "The first word in the deacons' list is also a 'cover' term, describing a kind of personal dignity that makes one worthy of respect."[4]

Like pastors, "deacons, as recognized leaders in the church, also had a high profile and thus were required to be worthy of respect (*semnous*). This is not the same term for respectability applied to the overseers (3:2). Here the term can mean 'serious' or 'honorable.'"[5] A deacon, like a pastor, must be a dignified individual who takes the ministry seriously.

Holding the Mystery of the Faith
With a Clear Conscience

Echontas to musterion tes pisteos en kathara suneidesei (1 Tim. 3:9). *Musterion* is the source of our English word "mystery," which is also the Greek literal meaning. The NIV has "deep truths," but that obscures the way Paul uses *musterion* in his epistles, where it always has the basic idea of something previously hidden but now revealed.

A biblical *mystery* is not something mysterious, obscure or unknown. Rather, it "refers to a truth, formerly hidden, but now revealed to those who will accept it by faith . . . In 1 Timothy 3:9 (KJV) it is the 'mystery of the faith,' the basic truth that constitutes the Christian faith (e.g. the incarnation, vicarious death, and bodily resurrection of Jesus Christ)."[6]

Suneidesei refers to "right conduct, free from guilt." God requires a deacon to hold the "mystery of the faith with a pure conscience." "A pure conscience indicates a pure life."[7]

Living belief is what Hughes calls "holding the mystery of the faith with a clear conscience." He says that what a deacon "understands must not only inform his life, but he must also live by it 'with a clear conscience.' A man's faith is in great shape when his conscience does not reproach the way he lives."[8]

Therefore, deacons must uphold the fundamentals of the Christian faith without compromise. Living in the light of these biblical doctrines will enable them to have a clear conscience. Mounce summarizes a deacon's *living belief* with these words: "Theology and morality can never be separated without fatal damage to either or both."[9]

Tested

Kai houtoi de dokimadzesthosan proton (1 Tim. 3:10). The KJV renders this phrase as "and these also let them be proved first." The word d*okimadzesthosan,* translated "proved" means "tested" or "examined." "Deacons are to be tried, investigated, and proved before they are asked to be deacons."[10]

Paul does not specify how the congregation is to carry out this testing. Some commentators emphasize the importance of observation, implying that the people in the church should observe a deacon candidate for an adequate length of time. In the course of this time, the congregation will be able to verify that this man has no disqualifying characteristics.

The verb for testing (*dokimzo*) means to test in the hope of being successful. Therefore, the pastor should provide ministry opportunities to men who may qualify as deacons to verify their character and ability to carry out tasks. Then the people can observe these men involved in serving and note their responses to various ministry challenges. Hughes says, "The pressures of their ministry would reveal what they were made of."[11]

A church should not elect a deacon who has had no practical ministry experience. Gutzke writes, "Just because a man means well, and just because he is genuine and sincere is not quite enough. Has he had any experience, and how would he get this experience? Give him other jobs to do, give him small jobs to do. If he shows himself to be a faithful man, he is qualified. If it turns out in the testing, examining, investigation, and looking over his past record, he is found to be above reproach, then let him serve as an officer of the church."[12]

The testing is not an official, rigorous examination, but rather it is an observation of the candidate's character. "The qualifications were principally of a character that could be recognized without any formal investigation."[13] Barton concurs: "This refers not to some formal testing but rather to observation by those who appoint deacons. The candidate will have shown the required moral characteristics and approved doctrine (3:9) consistently in the ordinary activities of church membership. A man who has proven his quality over time can then serve as a deacon. Testing deacons is needed today. They should not be appointed without consideration of their doctrine and their Christian life."[14]

Moreover, this testing of a deacon's consistent moral character testifies to his maturity. "In some churches today, the office of deacon has lost its importance. New Christians are often asked to serve in this position, but that is not the New Testament pattern. Paul said that potential deacons should be tested before they are asked to serve (3:10)."[15] The appointment of a deacon, as with an overseer, demands careful scrutiny. Having been tested and elected, the deacons must serve faithfully and joyfully.

Blameless

Anegkletoi (1 Timothy 3:10). *Egkletoi* means "called to account, reproveable, accused." The prefix *an* negates these qualities. The prospective deacon must be *un*impeachable, *un*reproveable, *un*accused. We find the same word in Titus 1:7 in Paul's list of pastoral qualifications. This term "specifies what the outcome of the testing must be before the potential candidates may enter into service as deacons. . . . [They] will be 'beyond reproach' or 'blameless' in the moral realm if a fair appraisal judges that they have each of the listed positive qualifications and none of the listed negative traits as characteristics in their lives."[16]

Chrysostom (John of Antioch), the great "golden mouthed" preacher of his age who lived about A.D. 400 said, "Observe how he [Paul] requires the same virtue from the deacons as from the bishops, for though they were not of equal rank, they must be equally blameless, equally pure."[17]

In 1 Timothy 3:2 Paul employs a synonym *anepilepton,* meaning "irreproachable." The KJV has "blameless," in all three cases (1 Tim. 3:2 & 10; Tit.1:7). Blamelessness "does not mean perfection, but outward flawlessness of walk."[18] Both a pastor and a deacon are to be men who live their lives above reproach. They must be men whose lives are of unimpeachable uprightness. God's standards for them are high indeed!

NOTES FOR
CHAPTER TWELVE

---

[1] Gutzke, *Plain Talk,* p 52.

[2] Knight, *Commentary on the Pastoral* Epistles, p. 168.

[3] Kent, *Pastoral Epistles,* p. 132.

[4] Fee, *1 and 2 Timothy, Titus,* p. 49.

[5] Bruce B. Barton, David R. Veerman, and Neil Wilson. *1 Timothy, 2 Timothy, Titus* in *Life Application Bible Commentary* (Wheaton, IL: Tyndale House Publishers, 1993), p. 66.

[6] Mounce, *Pass It On*, p. 43.

[7] Kent, *Pastoral Epistles*, p. 134.

[8] Hughes, *1 & 2 Timothy and Titus*, p. 85.

[9] Mounce, *Pass It On*, p. 43.

[10] Gutzke, *Plain Talk*, p.54.

[11] Hughes, *1 & 2 Timothy and Titus*, p. 86.

[12] Ibid., pp. 54-55.

[13] Ellicott, *Critical and Grammatical Commentary*, p. 47.

[14] Barton, *1 Timothy, 2 Timothy, Titus*, p. 68.

[15] Ibid., p. 67.

[16] Knight, *Commentary on the Pastoral Epistles*, p. 170.

[17] Chrysostom on "1 Timothy 3:12," in *Ancient Christian Commentary on Scripture*, p. 176.

[18] Hoste, *Bishops, Priests*, p. 134.

Chapter 13

DEACONESSES OR DEACONS' WIVES?

Introduction

In the middle of his qualifications for deacons, Paul inserts the following injunction: "Likewise, *their* wives must be reverent, not slanderers, temperate, faithful in all things" (1 Tim. 3:11). Before continuing with our discussion on deacons, we must take a moment and study Paul's words concerning these ladies in the congregation.

The Greek word rendered "wives" is *gunaikas,* which can be translated either as *women* or *wives.* The translation of this Greek term helps us identify the women that the Apostle Paul was admonishing.

Commentators propose several viewpoints on the identity of these women. The four most common views are the following: (1) They are women in general. (2) They are deaconesses who are deacons' wives. (3) They are a separate office of female deacons (that is deaconesses). (4) They are deacons' wives.

They Are Women in General

Some hold that Paul directed his admonition toward the women of the congregation in general. However, "This raises the question of why such a parenthesis would be inserted in the middle of Paul's list of qualifications for deacons."[1]

Commentators answer this question by stating that verse 12 contains material that the apostle tacked on as an afterthought. Fee says, "This verse is something of an afterthought. 'Oh yes, back to the deacon for a minute, he must be the husband of but one wife . . . and must manage his children and his household well.'"[2] However, the home life of the deacon was much too important for the apostle to treat it as an appendage.

Moreover, Paul's admonitions here in 1 Timothy 3:11 cannot refer to all the women in the church,[3] since the context of this chapter is about church officials. Instead, the last half of the previous chapter, 1 Timothy 2:9-15, contains Paul's instructions for all church women in general.

They Are Deaconesses Who Are Deacons' Wives

A few commentators believe that the women of verse 11 are those with a dual position. Mounce writes, "My suggestion is that the women in question are both the wives of the deacons and in some sense therefore deaconesses."[4]

Nonetheless, "Despite some good arguments, it is a stretch to read in deaconesses here because deacons are the focus mentioned on both sides of verse 11. It is natural, therefore, to view g*unaikas* as wives in its relationship to the deacons. Also, the Greek word that can be translated 'wife' or 'woman' has been translated 'wife' in verse 12 (the husband of one wife.)"[5] No commentator ever takes the view that verse 12 requires that a deacon must be "the husband of one deaconess!"

They Are Deaconesses

Many commentators argue that Paul's words in 3:11 refer to the office of deaconesses. Almost in lockstep, they propose the same arguments, some of which are briefly summarized below:

(1) The text does not have the word *their*. Translators have supplied it. Bassler says, "There is no possessive pronoun [*auton*], which would be expected if the reference were to 'their wives' (i.e., the deacons' wives)."[6]

(2) *Hosautos*, translated *even so* (KJV) and *likewise* (NKJV), seems to point to a class of people different than the bishops and deacons. The question is, "Which different class of people did Paul have in mind?" Bassler argues for deaconesses because *hosautos* refers to a group which is distinct from bishops and deacons.[7]

(3) Bassler also argues that "The order and parallelism of qualifications in ver. 8 and 11, coupled with the suitable change of *oilogous* to *diabolous* . . . and the moral requirements for the women here match those for the deacons in verse 8."[8] Thus, for Bassler, this match of requirements identifies the women as deaconesses.

(4) "If deacons' wives were meant we could have expected mention of overseers' wives following

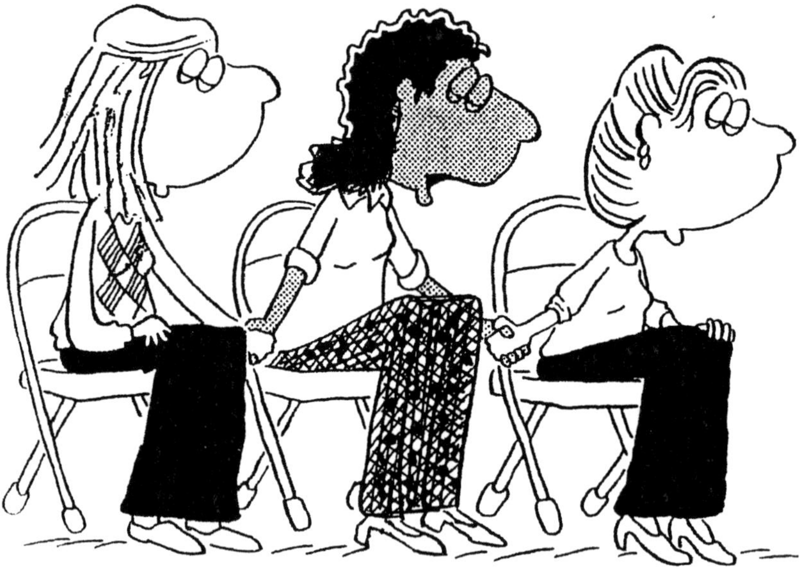

verse 7."[9] Since "Paul gave no qualifications for elders' wives. Why would he do so for deacons' wives?"[10]

(5) Some claim that there were women deacons in the churches of the apostolic period. For example, Bassler suggests this as one of her arguments: "Women are mentioned elsewhere in this role: Phoebe is specifically called 'deacon'; also Mary, Persis, Tryphena and Tryphosa (Romans 16); and Euodia and Suntyche (Philippians 4:2), whom Paul calls colleagues and members of the same team."[11]

(6) In 1 Timothy 3:11 "The word 'deacon' does not have a feminine form in the Bible and is used here like an adjective, 'deacons who are women.'"[12] MacArthur explains it this way, "Using the term women was the only way Paul could distinguish them from the male deacons."[13]

(7) In 3:11 Paul omits special notice of domestic duties of these women, whereas he lists these duties in the case of men. This indicates that Paul had deaconesses in mind here.

They Are Deacons' Wives

The term *gune* and its plural *gunaikos* have the general meaning of *woman* and *women* but often mean *wife* and *wives* as well. Both usages occur in the Pastoral Epistles, specially in 1 Timothy (*woman* occurs in 2:9, 10, 11, 12, 14, while *wife* occurs in 3:2; 12; and 5:9). Also, Barrett points out that Paul would have used a more explicit term than *women* if he had meant *deaconesses*, but he did not have to when referring to *wives*.[14]

Consequently, some consider these women only as the wives of deacons. One way to defend this view is to respond to each of the above arguments proposed by those who hold to deaconesses. Below are some brief responses to their arguments:

(1) The whole context of verses 8-13 is about deacons, so the original audience would have understood easily that *gunaikas* were the deacons' wives. Thus, the addition of the word *their* by the translators is an insignificant issue.

(2) Though *likewise* certainly indicates a group other than bishops and deacons, the distinct groups is not necessarily deaconesses, but simply deacons' wives. Women are different than men, so are wives different than husbands!

(3) We expect such an order and parallelism of qualifications in verses 8 and 11. Obviously, the moral standards and behavior of both deacons and their wives are equally important to Paul. A wife of low moral character disqualifies a man from the office of deacon.

Moreover, while some argue that the virtues demanded of the women in verse 11 would be irrelevant if only the wives of deacons were meant, their argument "is unconvincing, since the wives' activities and influence would not be limited to the kitchen and nursery."[15] "In one part of the deacons' office (care of sick and destitute) their wives might be fittingly associated with them. This is plausible."[16] The sick who needed to be visited certainly included women. The deacons also had the task of looking after the church's needy widows in their homes.

In that culture, it was unthinkable for a man to carry out this ministry by himself among women—a wife was essential in his ministry. Thus, Paul needed to outline qualifications for deacons' wives. Even Bassler, who left no verse unturned to find *deaconesses* in the New Testament, admits, "The placement of the verse—in the midst of a discussion of qualifications for men who would be deacons—lends support to their identification as wives."[17]

(4) Hanson appropriately explains why Paul set forth qualities for deacons' wives and not for bishops' wives: "Presumably the wife of a prospective bishop would be an older woman and therefore better known in the local church. Deacons might be more recently married and their wives unknown and perhaps more inclined to unsuitable behaviour."[18]

More importantly, God forbids a woman to teach and have authority over a man (1 Tim. 2:12). Thus, a bishop's wife may not partner with her husband in preaching, teaching, and ruling over the congregation. However, deacons' wives may partner with their husbands in their serving ministries—not as officiates, but simply as wives. "As spouses of the deacons they are to be involved with their husbands as their husbands seek to fulfill their diaconal service. The translation 'wives' expresses this unique relationship and responsibility."[19] Simply put, deacons were servants, and their wives were their fellow servants!

(5) The apostolic churches did not have women deacons. The office of deaconesses developed gradually and did not become an official order until about the middle of the third century.[20]

Thus, Phoebe (Rom. 16:1-2) did not hold the office of deaconess. The word *diakonon* in Romans 16:1 should be translated *servant* (as it is in the KJV, NKJV, and NASB). Moellering affirms, "Paul's designation of Phoebe as a deaconess (Rom. 16:1) [NLT] does not prove the existence of a definite office of deaconesses, since the term simply describes her as one who characteristically rendered conspicuous service in the congregation."[21]

The term *diakonos* is found twenty-six times in the New Testament. Outside of 1 Timothy 3, *diakonos* always is translated as *servant* or *minister* with the exception of a few modern versions, like the NLT, which assigns the title *deaconess* to Phoebe in Romans 16:1. Mary, Persis, Tryphena, and Tryphosa were not deaconesses. Paul **never** used the word *diakonos* in conjunction with these women, nor did he ever designate them as deaconesses. Mary (Romans 16:6) was one who "labored much" for Paul and his team. That does not make her a deaconess. Persis, Tryphena and Tryphosa all "labored in the Lord" (Romans 16:12) as did many church members who were not deacons.

Paul's description of Euodia and Syntyche clearly reveals that they were only his helpers. He calls them "women who labored with me in the gospel" (Phil. 4:3). The context has nothing to do with their official position as deaconesses in the church, but with their discord! "At one time Euodia and Suntyche contended at Paul's side in the cause of the gospel. But as he wrote they were not in harmony with each other. They were contentious, rather than content."[22] The apostle admonished them to put their discord behind them, so that unity could prevail in the Philippian congregation (Phil. 4:2).

(6) Paul did not use the term *gunaikas* (women) simply to distinguish them from the male deacons because he could not think of a feminine form for *diakonos*! The apostle could have added a feminine ending to *diakonos* had he desired to do so. It was not uncommon for Paul to make up new words to describe

people. For example, he coined new words when he admonished older women to teach younger women to be *philandrous*, literally husband-lovers, and *philoteknous*, children-lovers (Titus 2:4).

Later on, Christians made up the word *diakonissa* (Latin for deaconess). This term "did not come into use until the 4th cent.," and the office "which developed greatly in the 3rd and 4th cents. is described in the 'Didascalia' and the 'Apostolic Constitutions.'"[23] The title *diakonissa* thus came into being in post-biblical Greek.[24] Therefore, the obvious reason why the word *deacon* does not have a feminine form in the Bible is because the office of female deacons did not exist in the apostolic church. Paul is speaking about deacons' wives!

(7) The omission of any special notice of domestic duties is logical in I Timothy 3:11 because this portion deals with ministry. 1 Timothy 5:14 contains Paul's exhortation regarding the domestic duties of younger women.

One can turn this domestic argument around. If an official church office were in view here, then "a reference to deaconesses would have been more detailed; for example, it might have required that a deaconess be 'faithful to her one husband.'"[25]

Since Paul required faithfulness of an elder to his wife, why would Paul omit the issue of a deaconess' faithfulness to her husband if these women were deaconesses? The answer to this question is that these women did not have an official position in the church. "This omission is significant because this qualification is always mentioned in the PE [Pastoral Epistles] where positions of ministry or service are in view.[26]

Verse 11 fits in perfectly well in the midst of the criteria for deacons since it refers to deacons' wives.

Among the qualifications of a deacon is this one: that his wife must be a serious, godly woman. "There is immense common sense here not only as to the nature of marriage in which two become one, but in the strength that a godly couple will bring to a deacon's ministry. The character qualifications of deacons in verse 8 and the parallel qualifications for their wives in verse 11 insure that they will not only be mutually respectable but will have the same heart for ministry."[27]

After this three-fold description of the deacons' wives, Paul moves naturally into the next verse to say that the deacon must have only one wife, and that his children must be well behaved (v.12). It's all in the family!

NOTES FOR
CHAPTER THIRTEEN

[1] Mounce, *Pass It On*, p. 44.

[2] Fee, *1 and 2 Timothy, Titus*, p. 89.

[3] Kent, *Pastoral Epistles*, p. 136.

[4] Mounce, *Pass It On*, p. 44.

[5] Hughes, *1 & 2 Timothy and Titus*, p. 86.

[6] Jouette M. Bassler, *1 Timothy, 2 Timothy, Titus*, in *Abingdon New Testament Commentaries* (Nashville: Abingdon Press, 1996), p. 70.

[7] Ibid.

[8] Ibid.

[9] Michael Griffiths, *Timothy and Titus* (Grand Rapids: Baker Book House, 1996), p. 79.

[10] John MacArthur, *1 Timothy* in *The MacArthur New Testament Commentary* (Chicago: Moody Press, 1995), p. 130.

[11] Griffiths, *Timothy and Titus*, p. 80.

[12] Ibid.

[13] MacArthur, *1 Timothy*, p. 130.

[14] Barret, *The Pastoral Epistles*, p. 59.

[15] H. Armin Moellering, *1 Timothy, 2 Timothy, Titus* in the *Concordia Commentary* (Saint Louis: Concordia Publishing House, 1970), p. 75.

[16] Ellicott, *A Critical and grammatical Commentary*, citing Huther, p. 47.

[17] Bassler, *1 Timothy, 2 Timothy, Titus*, p. 70.

[18] Hanson, *The Pastoral Epistles*, p. 81.

[19] Knight, *Commentary on the Pastoral Epistles*, p. 171.

[20] Wayne H. House, *The Role of Women in Ministry Today* (Grand Rapids: Baker Books, 1995), p. 105.

[21] Moellering, *1 Timothy, 2 Timothy, Titus*, p. 75.

[22] Robert P. Lightner, "Philippians" in *The Bible Knowledge Commentary, New Testament Edition,* edited by John F. Walvoord and Roy B. Zuck (Wheaton, IL: Victor Books, 1983), p. 663.

[23] *The Oxford Dictionary of the Christian Church,* edited by F. L. Cross, "Deaconess" (Oxford: Oxford University Press, 1997).

[24] Marvin R.Vincent, *Word Studies in the New Testament* (Grand Rapids: Eerdmans, 1946), vol. 3, p. 176.

[25] Barrett, *The Pastoral Epistles,* p.61.

[26] Knight, *Commentary on the Pastoral Epistles,* p. 171.

[27] Hughes, *1 & 2 Timothy and Titus,* pp. 86-87.

Chapter 14

THE DEACON AND HIS FAMILY

The Husband of One Wife

Diakonoi estosan mias gunaikos andres (1 Tim. 3:12). A literal translation of this phrase is "Those who serve let (them) be of one-wife husbands." As we continue with the list of the qualifications of deacons, we come to 1 Timothy 3:12. Without question, verses 8 to 10 deal with the requirements for men who are prospective deacons. Verse 11 refers to women, and verse 12 returns to the subject of prospective deacons.

Those who regard the women of verse 11 as deaconesses see a disconnect between this verse and those before and after it. They say that Paul abandoned the deacons at the end of verse 10 and then returned to them in verse 12. Blasser, who thinks that verse 11 refers to deaconesses, says that with verse 12 "The author *returns* quickly to the topic of male deacons and continues the list of the qualifications for them."[1] (Italics added) However, "It is unlikely that a reference to deaconesses would be introduced between these small paragraphs."[2] These women, as we established in chapter 13, are simply deacons' wives.

"This understanding of *gunaikes* as 'wives' also provides the solution for the reference to *gunaikes* at this place in the pericope. If it is wives that are in view, then the verse fits here as another qualification necessary for one who would be deacon and who would conduct his ministry with his wife's assistance. Thus the wife's qualifications are part and parcel of his qualification for the office of *diakonos*."[3]

Taking verse 11 as another criteria for deacons—to have temperate, sober, non-gossiping wives—leads us naturally into verse 12, dealing with the deacons' marital relationship. "Paul then goes on to the deacon's fidelity to his wife and his children and thereby he completes the picture of his family life (v.12)."[4] 1 Timothy 3:8-13 is not a disjointed paragraph. On the contrary, it is an example of Paul's typical logical flow of thought.

The Bible is clear, "A deacon whose wife does not measure up to the same spiritual qualities required of *him*, is not to be chosen as a deacon. A man whose wife is bossy, a backbiter, and a tale-carrier, is not to be elected to the office of deacon"[5] (Italics in original).

This qualification for a deacon matches the one for overseers spelled out in verses 2, 4, and 5. Paul included it in the deacons' list for the same reasons. A man's relationship with his wife impacts his ministry whether he is a pastor or a deacon.

Hoste expresses well the importance of a man's wife in his ministry. "Some may wonder what a man's wife can have to do with his public ministry. The day will declare how many a testimony has been marred by an unspiritual wife, trying to pull the strings of the work of the Church. On the other hand, how many a servant of God has been sustained and encouraged in his service by a godly helpmeet who put first things first!"[6] Briley

The
Family
Man

states it succinctly: "Every man who has done well with a bad wife could have done excellent with a good one."[7]

A deacon's wife is a co-servant with her husband, especially in his ministry with the women and children. "Indeed, she will be expected to help him fulfill his duties."[8] Moreover, she can be a tremendous help by encouraging him, sharing his burdens and heartaches, and praying for him. "What a joy it is when a deacon and his wife are thus in complete and happy accord in the service of the Lord."[9]

A deacon, like the pastor, must be devoted to his wife and give her all the love and consideration that a wife deserves. "No other woman can have his affections maritally, mentally, or emotionally. His wife ought to occupy his full horizon. He must love her as he loves himself. . . . He rejects as treachery anything that would alter his loving focus. A one-wife man places his wife at the center of his heart."[10]

Could a single man qualify as a deacon? Yes. The apostle did not say that a deacon must be "a husband of a wife." Nevertheless, if he is married, which would usually be the case in Paul's culture, a deacon had to be the "husband of one wife."

As is true with a pastor, a deacon cannot be divorced. This is a matter that the congregation must investigate. Does divorce disqualify a man from service in the church completely? No! "When divorced and remarried persons are saved, they should rejoice in their salvation, and should serve the Lord faithfully in every way they can."[11] However, divorce biblically does disqualify a man from serving in the pastorate and in the deaconate. He must be a "one-wife man." After discussing the relationship of deacons and their wives,

Paul addresses the relation of deacons and their children, thereby completing the picture of the family life.

Ruling children and households well

Teknon kalos proistamenoi (1 Tim. 3:12). The literal rendering of this phrase is "children well ruling." In Greek the term *teknon* (children) comes first because Paul wanted to focus the deacons' attention on the object of their ruling responsibility—to rear children who fear God and obey His Word.

Like the bishop, a deacon must manage his own family well. However a significant difference exists between the command for a bishop (vs. 4-5) and the one for a deacon (vs. 12): Knight points out, "The one noteworthy difference is the absence of the concluding phrase of v. 4 and of the corresponding deduction in v. 5. Both the similarity and the difference are significant: The similarity indicates that the home is the proving ground of fidelity for all officers."[12] Verse 5 states, "for if a man does not know how to rule his own house, how will he take care of the church of God?" Knight then affirms that this difference indicates that the implication spelled out in v. 5 is not drawn for the *diakonoi* [*deacons*] because they are not *episkopoi*, overseers of the church.[13]

The way a deacon governs his home reveals his capacity for service in the church, not for ruling. "First Timothy 3:12 reveals the beauty that heaven endorses regarding the standard of home life that is required by the Lord of one serving in this office."[14] "No place is more indicative of a person's real Christian life character than his home."[15] Therefore, a man whose children are rebellious is disqualified to serve as a deacon.

NOTES FOR
CHAPTER FOURTEEN

[1] Bassler, *1 Timothy, 2 Timothy, Titus*, pp. 70-71.

[2] Barrett, *The Pastoral Epistles*, p. 61.

[3] Knight, *Commentary on the Pastoral Epistles*, p. 172.

[4] Ibid.

[5] Oliver B. Greene, *The Epistles*, p. 127.

[6] Hoste, *Bishops, Priests*, p 132.

[7] Briley, *The Deacon's Life*, p. 37.

[8] Hughes, *1 & 2 Timothy and Titus*, p. 86.

[9] Briley, *The Deacon's Life*, p. 37.

[10] Hughes, *1 & 2 Timothy and Titus*, p. 87.

[11] Oliver B. Greene, *The Epistles*, p. 127.

[12] Knight, *Commentary on the Pastoral Epistles*, p. 173.

[13] Ibid.

[14] Briley, *The Deacon's Life*, p. 32.

[15] Kent, *Pastoral Epistles*, p. 135.

Chapter 15

WHAT THE DEACONS' WIVES SHOULD BE

Introduction

Although the identity of the women in 1 Timothy 3:11 is disputed, it is best to view them as the wives of deacons. "Paul who was wise concerning sexuality . . . would propose the deacons' wives as their assistants."[1] The apostle set forth one negative quality that should not portray these wives and three positive traits that should characterize them. We will begin with the negative one.

Not Slanderers

Me diabolous. This plural adjective "slanderers" is found only in the Pastoral Epistles. This term refers to "the activity of 'malicious gossips' (NASB) or 'malicious talkers' (NIV). Here and in Titus 2:3 (with the identical construction) this concern is related specifically to women, but 2 Tim. 3:3 regards it as a problem of the day without regard to sexual identification."[2] The related singular noun *diabolos* (slanderer, devil) is what usually appears in the New Testament as in this chapter, verses 6 and 7, where it is correctly rendered "devil." "Satan is *the slanderer* par excellence. Women in the service of the church are not to be 'she-devils,' malicious scandalmongers."[3] Since their official duties would cause them to circulate among the congregation, they must avoid improper speech.[4]

Slandering is a destructive quality. "Nothing will tear a church apart quicker than busybodies who spend their time and energy carrying tidbits of information between members of the congregation."[5] John Calvin, the austere sixteenth century reformer, makes this snide observation about women and gossip: "Talkativeness is a disease of women, and it is increased by old age."[6] Wives of deacons must not be gossips. However, they must display the following godly characteristics.

Serious, Honorable

Semnas. This word is the feminine form of the same quality required of deacons in 1 Timothy 3:8. Paul also requires this trait of the older men in the Cretan church (*semnous* in Titus 2:2). The term means "noble, honorable, venerable, and serious." "Serious women are dignified, worthy of respect."[7] Since their actions and demeanor will make them worthy of this respect, deacons' wives must not be frivolous, but dignified.

Verse 11 begins with the word "likewise" as verse 8 does, taking us back to the overseers. God has a high standard for a bishop, deacons, and deacons' wives. Therefore, just as the deacons must be men who behave in a manner worthy of respect, "in the same way, their wives must be respected" (NLT).

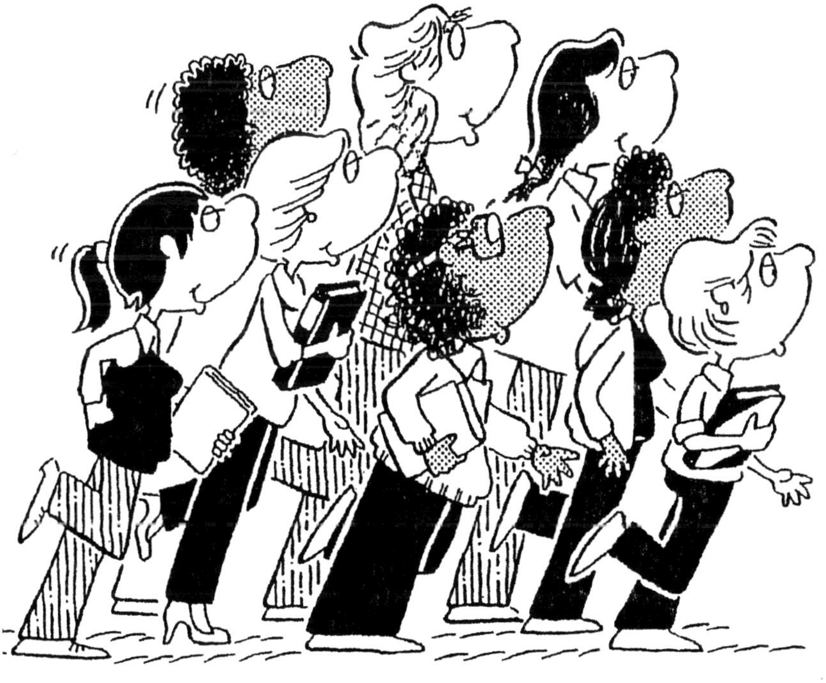

Sober

Nephalious. This word is also in the list dealing with the pastor (1 Tim. 3:2). The NKJV and NASB translate it "temperate" in both verses (3:2 and 3:11). Like the overseer, deacons' wives must be temperate. Although *nephalious* can mean "temperate in the use of alcoholic beverages," here it probably means "sober" in the sense of clear-headed, self-controlled.[8]

This character quality of self-control, tempers the entire life of a deacon's wife, including cultural fads. She "cannot be a product of the world and at the same time be an honorable instrument for the Lord."[9] Deacons' wives must be "marked by moderation and limits, not extreme or excessive, with an absence of extravagance."[10] Moreover, they must be able to think on their feet!

Faithful in all Things

Pistas en pasin. "Faithful in all things" is an important requirement for anyone who carries out many duties on behalf of the congregation. "A helper who constantly forgets to fulfill her duties or only does them halfway is not suitable for service in the church."[11] However, a deacon's wife who accomplishes her task joyfully is a blessing to the church.

The divine qualifications for deacons and their wives are similar and promote faithful service. Both husband and wife "are to be serious-minded, temperate and absolutely dependable."[12] However, the list of the qualifications for the wives of deacons does not mention that they must be tested and be above reproach. Knight provides a helpful explanation for the omission of this requirement for the wives. He makes this important statement: "It is not they, but their husbands, who are being elected to and put into office. Thus certain qualifications are left out of consideration, which thus in itself gives further corroboration to the conclusion that those in view in v. 11 are 'wives' who assist the διάκονοι, their husbands."[13]

A wife is an invaluable partner to a deacon! "A man is fortunate indeed when he marries a woman who possesses the qualities of a deacon's wife."[14]

NOTES FOR CHAPTER FIFTEEN

[1] Knight, *Commentary on the Pastoral Epistles*, p. 171.

[2] Ibid., p. 172.

[3] Mounce, *Pass It On*, pp. 44-45.

[4] Kent, *Pastoral Epistles*, p. 137.

[5] Mounce, *Pass It On*, p. 42.

[6] John Calvin, *Commentaries on the Epistles to Timothy, Titus, and Philemon* (Grand Rapids: Wm. B. Eerdmans Publishing, Co., 1948), p. 311.

[7] Barton, *1 Timothy, 2 Timothy, Titus*, p. 68.

[8] Knight, *Commentary on the Pastoral Epistles*, p. 159.

[9] Briley, *The Deacon's Life*, p. 39.

[10] Barton, *1 Timothy, 2 Timothy, Titus*, pp. 68-69.

[11] Ibid., p. 69.

[12] Mounce, *Pass It On*, p. 44.

[13] Knight, *Commentary on the Pastoral Epistles*, p. 173.

[14] Briley, *The Deacon's Life*, p. 36.

Chapter 16

THE DEACONS' REWARD FOR SERVING WELL

"For those who have served well as deacons obtain for themselves a good standing and great boldness in the faith which is in Christ Jesus" (1 Timothy 3:13). This verse indicates that faithful deacons will receive a reward that involves a good standing and great boldness.

Good Standing

The Greek word *bathmon* literally means a "step." It can also be translated "degree" (KJV) or "standing" (NKJV and NASB). Ellicott lists the three most commonly held views on the meaning of *bathmon*: (1) a "step" depicting an advance to a higher spiritual office; (2) a "post" referring to the honorable position a deacon occupied in the church; (3) a "degree" pointing to the deacon's reward at the Judgment Seat.[1]

A few commentators think that the reward is an advancement. They say that, after serving well as a deacon, a man would be promoted to the office of bishop (pastor). However, history does not show that this is what generally happened.

Hughes sees this reward as the deacon's special standing among the church members and explains why a deacon is worthy of his honorable position. Hughes does so with this nice summary of the deacon's biblical traits: "The deacon's life speaks. Because of his *elder-like* respectability, his *informed belief* as he holds the mystery of the faith, his *living belief* that issues in 'a clear conscience,' his *tested* life oozes with character. His *help-mate* is his best qualification, and he is graciously *domesticated* in relation to his wife and children. All of this provides him an excellent standing with his people. His authority goes far beyond words."[2]

Moellering believes *bathmon* refers to a step that brings him closer to God and puts and interesting twist on it by going way back to Genesis and introducing Jacob's ladder into the whole subject! He says, "Perhaps it is better to think in terms of the Old Testament picture of a ladder leading to heaven (Gen. 28). The word for 'standing' in the original literally means 'step.' As he faithfully exercises the duties of his office, the deacon feels himself graciously elevated closer to God, and in His nearer presence a bolder conscience pervades his soul, inspiring him to a more fearless testimony and enabling him to look forward without terror to the Day of Judgment."[3]

MacArthur provides a good explanation of *bathmon* in relation to deacons. He writes, "First, they obtain for themselves a high standing *bathmos* (standing). Here it is used metaphorically to speak of those who are a step above everyone else. In our vernacular, we might say they are put on a pedestal. That is not sinful pride, because deacons do not seek it, yet are worthy of it."[4]

MacArthur then adds, "The deacons who serve well will get a two-fold reward—before man and before God. Those who serve in humility will be exalted by God (James 4:10; 1 Peter 5:6), and by the church (1 Thess. 5:12-13). Faithful deacons will be respected and honored by those they serve. It is only by commanding such respect that deacons can be examples, since respected people are the ones emulated."[5]

Great Boldness

Parresian means "boldness," "assurance," or "great confidence." This word is often used of boldness of speech (cf. Acts 4:13). "Boldness seems primarily towards man, though it could include the notion of boldness in approach to God."[6]

A godly deacon is able to speak boldly of his faith and serve faithfully, knowing that his divine Master appreciates and values what he does. Stephen, one of the original seven deacons, confidently proclaimed his faith in Christ unto death. Stephen prayed to his sympathetic Master with full assurance: "Lord Jesus, receive my spirit" (Acts 7:59). Stephen's martyrdom gave rise to a great persecution against the Jerusalem believers, causing them to scatter. One of them was Philip, another of the original seven deacons. He did not go into hiding, but pioneered the field of Samaria and with great assurance preached Christ to the Samaritans (Acts 8:5 ff.).

"When a deacon has indeed 'served well,' his ministry builds confidence in the sincerity of his own faith in Christ and of his unhypocritical approach to God (cf. Eph.. 3:12; Heb. 10:19)."[7] As Kent reminds us, this boldness has immediate and future benefits: "Deacons who perform well have as a consequence real confidence in the sphere of their Christian faith. They can approach God boldly in prayer, knowing that no sin or carelessness in spiritual matters is barring the way. Such spiritual boldness or confidence will also assist them in further spiritual labors." [8] This should encourage deacons to fulfill their office conscientiously.

NOTES FOR
CHAPTER SIXTEEN

[1] Ellicott, *A Critical and Grammatical Commentary*, p. 48.

[2] Ibid.

[3] Moellering, *1 Timothy, 2 Timothy, Titus*, p. 76.

[4] MacArthur, *1 Timothy*, p. 313.

[5] Ibid.

[6] Donald Guthrie, *The Pastoral Epistles*, p. 98.

[7] A. Duane Litfin, "1 Timothy" in *The Bible Knowledge Commentary, New Testament Edition*. Edited by John F. Walvoord and Roy B. Zuck (Wheaton, IL: Victor Books, 1983), p. 738.

[8] Kent, *Pastoral Epistles*, p. 138.

Part Three

The Roles and Relationships of the Pastor and Deacons

Chapter 17

THE PASTOR'S SCRIPTURAL ROLES

In his book, *You Can't Lose For Winning: A Candid Look at Minister, Layman and Church in a Changing World,* Jess C. Moody claims, "The ministry is indeed the worst profession; but, under God's calling, it is fantastically thrilling."[1] Some veteran pastors may agree with this paradox.

Moody also states with tongue in cheek: "The synonym for pastor is wet-nurse."[2] Perhaps there is some truth in Moody's words since today's pastor needs to spend so much time counseling and helping people with their personal problems. This leads us to ask the question, "What are the Scriptural roles of a Pastor?"

Before answering this question, we must review briefly the three New Testament words that refer to a pastor: *presbuteros* (elder), *episkopos* (bishop), and *poimen* (shepherd). We come across a reference to all three in Peter's exhortation to elders (1 Pet. 5:1-4), and in Luke's account of Paul's farewell to the Ephesian elders (Acts 20:17-28).

The Apostle Peter wrote, "To the **elders** which are among you" (v.1), and he exhorted them with these words: "**Shepherd** the flock of God which is among you, serving as **overseers**" (v. 2).

Luke wrote, "From Miletus Paul sent to Ephesus, and called the **elders** of the church" (v. 17). Then Paul said to them, "Therefore take heed to yourselves and to all the flock, among which the Holy Spirit has made you **overseers**, to **shepherd** the church of God which He purchased with His own blood" (v. 28).

Elder indicates *maturity*; **overseer** pertains to *administration*; and **shepherd** speaks of *pastoral care*. What are the roles of this elder/bishop/pastor? The roles of this mature man are two-fold: (1) As a bishop he is to oversee the ministries of the church, and (2) as a shepherd he is to care for the congregation.

Of course, since these roles are of one and the same person, they are interrelated. For example, his duty to lead arises from his overseeing and shepherding roles. His teaching and preaching duties relate to his shepherding and overseeing roles—he feeds believers to equip them for service in the church. Also, since a pastor must be a mature believer, he should be able to provide godly counsel, which fulfills his shepherding role. To achieve his God-given roles, a pastor must carry out several duties. Let us look at some of these.

His Duties as a Shepherd

To Provide Food for the Flock

A pastor fulfills this duty by teaching and preaching the Word of God to the flock. All three Pastoral Epistles address the importance of the pastor's teaching and preaching ministry. 1 Timothy 3:2 tells us

Today our lesson is……

that a bishop must be "able to teach." 2 Timothy 2:2 gives us the Apostle's exhortation to Timothy, who was the pastor of the Ephesian church. Paul said to him, "And the things that you have heard from me among many witnesses, commit these to faithful men who will be able to teach others also."

Moreover, in 2 Timothy 4:2 we find Paul's urgent command to Timothy: "Preach the Word! Be ready in season and out of season. Convince, rebuke, exhort, with all longsuffering and teaching." Then in the midst of the requirements that Paul laid down for an elder, Paul told Titus that a bishop must be one "holding fast the faithful word as he has been taught, that he may be able by sound doctrine both to exhort and to convict those who contradict" (Titus 1:9).

The Apostle Paul encouraged Timothy regarding his teaching responsibility with these words: "If you instruct the brethren in these things, you will be a good minister of Jesus Christ, nourished in the words of faith and of the good doctrine which you have carefully followed." This dual task of teaching and preaching requires that a pastor feed on the Word. "A good diet makes a good minister. The most effective ministers have been those who persevered as students of the Word."[3]

Paul is an excellent example of a student of the Word. As he awaited execution in a cold, dark dungeon, he asked Timothy to bring a warm coat and also some books, specially the parchments—these were manuscript copies of the Hebrew Scriptures. Paul was an earnest student of the Word to his dying day (2 Timothy 4:13).

One summer I was down in Dallas, Texas, studying as a graduate student in library science at a nearby university. Our first Sunday in Dallas, my wife and I visited a Baptist Church across the street from our apartment. When we walked in, we found ourselves in the midst of a cheerful congregation, celebrating its new pastor's first Sunday.

The pastor began his message by stating that he could come up with a sermon in fifteen minutes. I wondered how he could accomplish this in such a short time—it takes me an average of eight hours to prepare a message! The pastor prattled for an hour, evidencing his lack of diligence in the study of the Word. I never forgot his opening remark. The next Sunday we visited another Baptist church in the area and sat under sound Bible teaching; we attended there through the summer.

The following summer when we returned to Dallas to continue my studies, I said to my wife, "Let's go back to the first church to see how it is going." We were surprised to see how small the congregation was, but we were blessed by the sermon of a brand new pastor. After the service, I asked one of the men from the church about their former pastor and received this response, "That man was not a pastor! He was a con-artist who nearly killed our church. So we recently made him resign." Thankfully their new pastor was a student of the Word.

God has given me the opportunity to teach Bible college and seminary pastoral students. I often remind them that if they do not like to study, they should not go into the pastorate. It takes time to be a student of the Word and prepare messages. This account by Dawson reminds us of the numerous messages a pastor must prepare: "A non church-goer friend of mine was amazed the other day to learn that denominations do not send out to their ministers the sermons they are to preach. He was quite sure it was not possible for anyone to conceive of a sermon outline, develop, illustrate and preach it without outside help. Then when he heard that the average minister has to develop two sermons for Sunday, at least one other during the week, and funeral sermons, talks to committees, and other groups, he was sure I was a liar."[4] Dawson was not lying; he was telling it like it is!

To be a student of Scripture is truly a challenge. It requires much preparation, week after week, to preach fresh sermons that God uses to change lives. As believers respond to the teaching and preaching of the Word, they grow in the faith and become more Christlike. Then the pastor will not have to spend so much time solving personal problems among the people in the congregation.

To Provide Care, Guidance and Protection for the Flock

In Bible times, caring for sheep was a humble vocation. Often because a shepherd spent so much time with his sheep, he himself would begin to smell like the animals under his care. Thus, his sheep knew him well, and he knew them so well that he could call each one by name (cf. John 10:3). He did not drive his sheep, but they trustingly followed his lead—not that of a stranger whose voice they did not know. A shepherd nursed the sheep that were sick, and he bound up the broken limbs of those that had fallen or had encountered predators. He led them to cool waters and green pastures, and he guarded them from all danger (Ps. 23:2; Jn. 10:11-12).

This description of a shepherd in Bible times helps us understand why Jesus compared Himself to a shepherd. He proclaimed, "I am the good shepherd. The good shepherd gives His life for his sheep" (Jn. 10:11). His sacrificial care led Him to a cruel death on the cross.

The gentle Good Shepherd, who sacrificially cared for His sheep, is the example that a pastor must follow. Therefore, he should never lord over the church but lead by example (1 Pet. 5:3). People often do foolish things and stray; the pastor must lead them back, not drive them. When a sinning believer refuses to repent, a loving pastor will take the disciplinary steps that lead to restoration into the fold. Love, humility, sacrifice must mark a biblical pastor as he cares for the congregation.

"Unfortunately, some pastors isolate themselves from their people because they have adopted an inaccurate idea of their position. They think of themselves as prophets, for example, and therefore picture themselves on a hill, thundering down to the crowds below. They don't have a loving congregation as much as a trembling audience."[5]

In contrast, a pastor should strive to become well acquainted with his people by spending time with them. One way is to visit them in their homes. He also should call on the sick frequently and should seek to mend those who are hurting spiritually by providing them godly counsel.

Thus, his visitation rounds must include Bible reading and prayer. This affords him the one-on-one opportunity to teach and exhort his people to live godly lives, regardless of their circumstances. This personal ministry is effective when the pastor carries it out in a firm but loving manner. Moreover, through this informal teaching a pastor is able to warn his people against any false teaching that may be preying on them.

His Duties as an Overseer

To Lead the Church Ministries

As the bishop of a congregation, the pastor is the administrator of the church. "Contrast the term deacon, meaning a servant, with the term for pastor, bishop or overseer. The pastor was to 'rule . . . the church of God' (I Tim 3:4-5)."[6]

It seems strange in our day to call Pastor Smith, "Bishop Smith." However, in the early New Testament church, "bishop" was one of the titles for a pastor because it emphasized his administrative duties, which required leadership. Pastors may fall into a variety of leadership styles. Let us examine a few of them.

The Non-Leader Pastor

On one extreme is the "non-leader" pastor. "No matter how much he may protest the role, the patent fact is that *his people expect him to lead.* I have seen church after church collapse under the ministry of the 'whatever you men say' type of pastor. Whenever an opportunity comes to make a decision, a real leadership decision, he wrings his hands and meekly says, 'whatever you men say.'"[7] (Italics in original)

The pastor who is a "doormat" will soon find his leadership role destroyed. This is the type of man who will never stand up for anything because he is afraid he will offend one of his church lay leaders. He needs to remember that "The pastor is not the hired man of the church, subject to all the whims of the members."[8] He is a man whom God has called to lead the members as they serve in the local church!

Moreover, weak pastoral leadership damages the congregation. "A church with frail, frightened leadership will disintegrate because several vacuums will be created and the dynamic lay leaders of the church will fill them rather than see the church die. The next situation that evolves is that these laymen will develop a rivalry between the leadership groups. If the pastor won't lead, they will. Then problems become severely acute."[9]

The Domineering Pastor

On the opposite extreme is the autocratic leadership style. Cobb states, "I have seen some—not many, thank the Lord—who have given orders to the laymen as though they were soldiers receiving Orders of the Day, and who become furious if the orders were not carried out to the letter."[10] This type of pastor has earned the title of "Dictator." He also does great harm to a church. Laymen will not follow a tyrant for long. A pastor "has no biblical right to be autocratic, dictatorial or domineering. No man of God filled with the Spirit, will manifest such an attitude."[11]

A pastor must remember that "His authority in the church, as God's leader, is a moral and spiritual power, not a legal one. He should exercise leadership. He must refuse to compromise biblical convictions, even though he should be gracious in attitude, and never stubborn about personal opinions or desires that do not involve biblical principles. His authority rests in the power of a godly example, as well as in the fact that he is a biblical officer (1 Pet. 5:3; Eph. 4:11, 12). However, he is not to be a lord 'over God's heritage' (1 Pet. 5:1-4)."[12]

A pastor must lead not according to the world's philosophy but must be consistent with Christ's view.

Our culture "equates leadership with prestige, power and respect. This was not Christ's view of 'leadership.' His outlook on service for the kingdom was one of being other-centered rather than self-centered."[13]

The Good Leader

Between the two extremes is the good pastoral leader. Moody lays out what I would call the "Ten Commandments" of good leadership:
1. Never make an issue of things that are unimportant.
2. Always plan each program thoroughly.
3. Explain the plan as thoroughly as possible.
4. Anticipate every question or objection.
5. Enlist the support of your church leadership.
6. Show how the plan will advance the spiritual life of the church toward its larger goals.
7. Learn to live with compromise (not spiritual or moral).
8. Always put your relationship to your people above any program.
9. Never allow your ego to become affixed to any plan.
10. Break each particular program into small bits of possibility.[14]

To these I would add an eleventh commandment:
11. After the completion of a project or endeavor, always seek to recognize those who have contributed to the success of the endeavor.

At this point, we must emphasize that in order for a man to fulfill his pastoral leadership, he must evidence the qualities set forth in the New Testament, especially his ability to rule his own family. This is what Paul taught clearly when he said, "For if a man does not know how to rule his own house, how will he take care of the church of God?" (1 Tim. 3:5).

"Leaders, then, are to possess the kinds of qualities, which were generally admired in Graeco-Roman society. They are to be householders who run their households well, with subservient children, and who would play the same role in the churches. They are to be moderate men in control of their passions. They provide models for other male householders in the churches."[15]

The Visionary Leader

A good pastor should also be a visionary. As the leader he should be one who can dream great things for God, yet he must not be a wild dreamer. Rather, he must tame his vision by reality and common sense. "The open secret of ministerial leadership is that laymen love to follow their pastor. They want to do it and will, unless his leadership is absolutely without sense."[16]

Dreams only become reality if they are followed by sound, workable planning and planning must be followed by action. At the same time, a pastor must bathe the whole matter in prayer, humbly trusting God to accomplish His will.

To Equip the Church Members

This duty of the pastor clearly relates not only to his oversight role, but also to his shepherding one. Paul reminded the Ephesian believers that God had provided them gifted leaders, including pastors and teachers "for the equipping of the saints for the work of the ministry, for the edifying of the body of Christ, till we all come to the unity of the faith and of the knowledge of the Son of God, to a perfect man, to the measure of the stature of the fullness of Christ" (Eph. 4:12-13).

One of the pastor's biblical roles is to train believers for service. It is also his duty to delegate ministry responsibilities to these equipped members. "We are called as overseers to shepherd God's flock, equipping them to use their gifts to meet the needs of the body. A pastor can't and doesn't have to do it all."[17]

At the same time, the members of the church must be willing to assist in the ministry. God has endowed every member with the ability to serve in the church (1 Cor. 12). Thus, a pastor as the leader must ensure, as much as possible, that every member has the opportunity to serve. Participation of many members results in a healthy, vibrant congregation.

From time to time, as pastor of Maranatha Baptist Church, I would take a survey to see where each member was ministering. It was a joy to learn that eighty-five percent of the adult members, men and women, were involved in some area of service in the church. I praised God for them and prayed for His continual work in the lives of all of us.

We must remember that the immediate goal of the pastor's equipping the saints is to edify the body of Christ. The ultimate purpose of training them is to glorify God by reflecting Christ to others. The Spirit helps us do this individually and as a congregation.

How Should the Church Membership Relate to the Pastor?

As we conclude this chapter on the roles of the pastor, we should take a look at what the Scriptures say regarding the congregation's relationship to the pastor.

Bible Study

According to the Scriptures, a pastor who faithfully fulfills his roles of leading and teaching the Word is worthy to receive double honor from his congregation. This is what Paul wrote to Timothy: "Let the elders that rule well be counted worthy of double honor, especially those who labor in the word and doctrine. For the Scripture says, 'You shall not muzzle an ox while it treads out the grain,' and 'The laborer is worthy of his wages'" (1 Tim 5:17-18; see also 1 Cor. 9:14). Consequently, one facet of this double honor is an adequate salary. A good rule of thumb is the average of what the members of the congregation earn.

The Apostle Paul then wrote these words related to this subject of honoring pastors: "Do not receive an accusation against an elder except from two or three witnesses. Those who are sinning rebuke in the presence of all, that the rest also may fear" (1 Tim. 5:19-20).

Besides the honor of fitting wages, another aspect of the double honor is protection from false accusations (1 Tim. 5:19). When people have minor grievances with the pastor, they should approach him privately about the matter. A pastor should never be the object of public criticism in minor details or incidents. Members must refrain from correcting in public a pastor's insignificant mistakes. However, when serious accusations arise against a pastor, a congregation must follow biblical principles in dealing with these severe allegations against him (cf. Matt. 18:15-20).

Protecting the pastor from false accusations is "important for the morale of the whole congregation. People will talk; and some people will believe the worst they hear, and will repeat it. Such gossip is injurious to everyone, to the person being talked about and the person who is doing the talking. The elder stands out in front and above, and he is an easy target. Remember that the minister is the teaching elder. Here is a thought for us to have in mind; the leader, the minister, the elder, the preacher, needs protection and deserves protection."[18]

Moreover, a pastor is worthy of respect. Paul's exhortation to the Thessalonian believers brings this out: "And we urge you, brethren, to recognize those who labor among you, and are over you in the Lord and admonish you, and to esteem them very highly in love for their work's sake, and be at peace among yourselves" (1 Thess. 5:12-13). One practical way to esteem the pastor highly is to speak of him and address him by his title. Out of respect, no member should call a pastor by his first name.

Finally, the lay leaders and other church members must submit to the leadership of the pastor. Following is the biblical command to believers regarding this matter: "Obey them that rule over you, and be submissive, for they watch out for your souls, as those who must give account. Let them do so with joy and not with grief, for that would be unprofitable for you" (Heb. 13:17).

NOTES FOR
CHAPTER SEVENTEEN

[1] Jess C. Moody, *You Can't Lose For Winning: A Candid Look at Minister, Layman and Church in a Changing World* (Grand Rapids: Zondervan Publishing House, 1965), p. 91.

[2] Ibid., p 31.

[3] Hughes, *1 & 2 Timothy and Titus*, p. 107.

[4] Dawson, David Miles, *More Power to the Preacher* (Grand Rapids: Zondervan Publishing House, 1956), p. 62.

[5] E. Glenn Wagner and Steve Halliday, *Escape From Church, Inc.* (Grand Rapids: Zondervan, 1999), p. 132.

[6] John R. Rice, *God's Work: How to Do It* (Murfreesboro, TN: Sword of the Lord, 1971), p. 56.

[7] Moody, *You Can't Lose*, p. 58.

[8] Jackson, *The Doctrine and Administration*, p. 42.

[9] Moody, *You Can't Lose*, pp. 58-59.

[10] Ibid., p. 59.

[11] Briley, *The Deacon's Life*, pp. 23-24.

[12] Ibid. p. 23.

[13] House, *The Role of Women*, p. 184.

[14] Moody, *You Can't Lose*, p. 60.

[15] Margaret Davies, *The Pastoral Epistles* (Sheffield, England: Sheffield Academic Press, 1996), p. 81.

[16] Moody, *You Can't Lose*, pp. 58-59.

[17] Wagner, *Escape From Church*, p. 110.

[18] Gutzke, Plain *Talk*, p. 90.

Chapter 18

THE DEACONS' SCRIPTURAL ROLE

To learn about the deacons' role we go to the New Testament, God's ministry description handbook. Every deacon should be acquainted with the Scriptures dealing with his role. "Many men who have had the responsibilities of the deaconship imposed upon them by the churches fail in their duties perhaps largely because of their lack of information; but that is altogether inexcusable, for they have the New Testament, which is the highest and most authentic source of information available."[1]

One thing is certain. The local church members elect their deacons to serve. Deacons should not consider themselves elected officials who govern the affairs of the church, nor should they look upon their office as an opportunity for self-aggrandizement. "The deaconship is degraded when it is sought for the sake of honor rather than service"[2] "The deacon is to serve meekly in the church, not with unruly spirit or in selfish pride."[3] Naylor in his book entitled, *The Baptist Deacon*, says, "The deacon is a servant of the church."[4] The basis for Naylor's remark lies in the term "deacon." Our English word "deacon" is a transliteration of the Greek word *diakonos*; it means *servant*. "Its use suggests that leadership is conceived as service to God and the community."[5] Although deacons' ministries consisted of service in the early church, Scripture does not make clear what their responsibilities were, nor does it specify what their relationship to the pastor was. Some people have come to the conclusion that deacons must be business men, and that the more successful and aggressive they are in the business world, the better qualified they are to fill the position of deacon. The false assumption that deacons must be businessmen rests upon the word *business* in Acts 6:3.

The term "business" in this verse is a rendering for the Greek word *chreias*, which means "need." The KJV and NKJV use this basic meaning twenty-five times in the New Testament.[6] Acts 6:3 is the only place where these two versions render it as "business." The NASB translates it "task" which is preferable.

The task of Stephen and the other six early deacons was to meet the needs of the Greek speaking widows. Cobb explains their role well. He says, "The primary duties of deacons are implied in the reasons for the institution of the office. Their chief function is to look after the temporal welfare of a church."[7]

1 Timothy 3 helps us understand that the role of deacons is different than that of a bishop. Paul's mention of the bishop's office and the deacons' office in the same passage points out a close relationship between these two offices. However, the term "deacon," which means "servant," indicates that the role of this office is somewhat below that of a "bishop," who is the overseer of the congregation.

Moreover, "in the list of qualifications for the office of deacon, 'apt teacher' is omitted. The strong term, 'not greedy for gain' (different from 'no lover of money' in the case of the bishop, v. 3) hints at access to congregational funds. In view of all this it seems safe to conclude that the deacon served in some supervisory, executive position in caring for the poor and probably the sick."[8]

Jackson gives the following well-defined description of what the role is for today's deacons, "It shall be the duty of the deacons to assist the pastor in promoting the spiritual welfare of the church; to be his helpers and counselors; to exercise prudent watchcare over the church membership; to seek out such members as need alms; to visit the sick; to examine with the pastor candidates for church membership; to assist at baptism, their wives assisting the ladies; and to supervise the preparation and distribution of the Lord's Supper."[9]

Incidentally, though in our churches we often see the deacons helping the pastor by distributing the bread and the cup during the Lord's Supper, Scripture does not list this activity as one of the deacons' duties, but neither does it forbid it. This practice "was adopted, it seems, as a convenience rather than as an enjoined duty."[10]

As deacons we are not to rule the church, but we must be sensitive to its concerns. Accordingly, deacons should stay in touch with the people and not disregard completely the wishes of the congregation. I remember one pastor and deacons' meeting when one deacon suggested a certain course of action in a church matter. Another deacon stated that the issue was of such a nature that that we should present it to the congregation for their approval. Then one of the other deacons said, "No, they may vote against us." I replied, "If we really believe in congregational government, we should not exclude the membership in a case like this." Thankfully, the deacons voted to take it to the church members for their input.

We may conclude from Acts 6:1-4 that the deacons' main role is to help the pastor by serving the church community. The deacons' assistance affords the pastor the time he needs to pray and to study God's Word, which are essential activities in the life of every godly leader. Deacons should uphold their pastor in prayer, giving him counsel, and being loyal to him. Deacons should also serve as the eyes and ears of the pastor by keeping him informed concerning the needs in the church community.

"In First Timothy 3:1-12 is revealed the most beautiful picture of how deacons should conduct themselves at church, at home, and in society. At church, the deacon was appointed and ordained to assist the pastor in making the ministry reach its total aim."[11]

Term of Office

One question that arises concerning the role of deacons is their term of office. Some people think that a deacon should hold the office for life. They contend that if a man meets the biblical qualifications, the church should not limit the length of his service. Others believe that the office should have term limits.

A study of Acts 6 implies that qualification does not necessarily result in election. In other words, just because a man is biblically qualified to be a deacon does not mean that a congregation must elect him to serve. Acts 4:4 indicates that the infant Jerusalem church had a large membership, which included five thousand men.

Out of that great number, surely more than just seven of those men met the biblical qualifications to be elected as deacons. However, the Jerusalem church chose only seven. In addition, Philip, one of the seven, was not a deacon for life for he moved away to Caesarea (cf., Acts 21:7). Consequently, he was no longer even a member of the local church in Jerusalem.

Electing deacons for life has undesirable results. "It has been the practice of many churches to elect deacons for life, and the general result has been to favor inefficiency and to promote incapacity."[12]

This account by Agar confirms the need for term limits: "The life-tenure has produced some very curious results. For instance, a local church elected a deacon for life. About seven years later the man moved to another city and caused the clerk to put a footnote on his church letter saying that he was a deacon. When the new church received the man by letter, he demanded to be recognized as a deacon because the other democracy had elected him a deacon for life. He was much incensed when it refused to do so."[13] To make such a demand goes against the autonomy of the local church.

Moreover, a deacon who holds the office for life may become proud and domineering and even possessive of his position. Dismissing such a man from the diaconate is a difficult task that may lead to a church split! Rotating church officers and committeemen is a wise policy to follow in administering church affairs. It gives more people an opportunity to serve the Lord. Rotation of officers also allows faithful men a time of rest and renewal.

Deacons who live up to their Scriptural role and serve well during their term of office are a blessing to any church. They will receive a reward from God at the

Bema seat of Christ. They may look forward to their Lord's commendation, "Well done, good and faithful servant; you were faithful over a few things, I will make you ruler over many things. Enter into the joy of your lord" (Matt. 25:21). Praise the Lord for godly deacons!

NOTES FOR
CHAPTER EIGHTEEN

[1] Cobb, *Cobb's Baptist Church Manual*, p. 76.

[2] Burroughs, *Honoring the Deaconship*, p. 11.

[3] Briley, *The Deacon's Life*, p. 43.

[4] Naylor, *The Baptist Deacon*, p. 21.

[5] Davies, *The Pastoral Epistles*, p. 80.

[6] Naylor, *Baptist Deacon*, p. 20.

[7] Cobb, *Church Manual*, p. 71.

[8] Moellering, *1 Timothy, 2 Timothy, Titus*, p. 74.

[9] Jackson, *The Doctrine and Administration*, p. 172.

[10] Cobb, *Church Manual*, pp. 75-77.

[11] Briley, *The Deacon's Life*, pp. 23-24.

[12] Agar, *Deacon at Work*, p. 12.

[13] Ibid., pp. 12-13.

Chapter 19

RIGHT RELATIONSHIPS

Jesus Christ, speaking of the Church Universal, said, "On this rock I will build my Church." (Mat. 16:18). The Church has a special place in the heart of our Lord Jesus Christ—it is infinitely dear to Him. He loved it so much that He "gave Himself for it" (Eph. 5:25). Christ's Church began at Pentecost, and He will continue to build it until He comes for it at the Rapture!

The local church also has a special place in the plan of God. 1 Timothy 3:15 refers to the local church as "the house of God, which is the church of the living God, the pillar and ground of the truth." 1 Timothy 3 also sets forth the qualifications of the only two biblical offices of the local church: the pastor and deacons. "These are two divinely-appointed offices in the New Testament church and were set up for the watch-care of the membership. The church will only progress in the work of the Lord as these two offices harmonize their efforts."[1]

Therefore, it is imperative that the pastor and the deacons of a local church take seriously their biblical roles, and that they seek to be at peace with one another. A right relationship between the pastor and the deacons will benefit the church and please the Lord.

"The pastor is the elected leader of the church. The office of deacon has been created to give assistance to the pastor. There is an interrelation between the two offices."[2] This bond is possible only if each person respects the other and stays within his God-given role.

Pastoring Maranatha was a blessing because of the many dedicated men who served as deacons. Among them was David Lord, who truly imitated his Savior's servant heart. David served his country—as a brave military man in the Army National Guard, his state—as a conservative representative and state senator, and his church—as a faithful deacon. He also served as a board member of several mission agencies, including Alpha Women's Center, a crisis pregnancy center in Des Moines, Iowa.

Regardless of his position, David served with a humble heart. When I asked the deacons to watch over various aspects of the ministry, such as visitation, buildings and grounds, or missions, David was willing to step in and serve in whatever area I assigned to him.

He was also a man of some means, but he never used his resources to elevate himself in the church or to push his own agenda. He was a man full of wisdom who gave me godly advice in a kindly way. We had a wonderfully close relationship. He often said, "Pastor, I pray for you every single day."

David had battled cancer before he and his family joined Maranatha, but under medical treatment the cancer had gone into remission. It crushed our hearts when the cancer returned and struck David again. We suffered through it together as friend with friend. His last words to me were, "Pastor, I love you." My last words to him were, "David I love you, too."

Pastor and deacon—brothers in Christ—a God honoring relationship—serving the church together!

NOTES FOR
CHAPTER NINETEEN

[1] O'Donnell, *Handbook for Deacons*, p. 53.

[2] Ibid.

Appendices

A Tribute to Pastors
and
Women's Ministries

Appendix A

A Tribute to Pastors

Hebrews 13:7-8, 17

The pastor of a small church in Detroit thought that some practical joker was ribbing him when IOUs began to appear in the collection plate. Then a few weeks later, an envelope turned up in the offering, which contained bills equal to the total of the IOUs.

After that, the preacher could hardly wait to see what amount the anonymous donor had promised. The notes ranged between $5 and $15, apparently based on what the donor thought the sermon was worth. This continued for some time. Then there was one Sunday when the note read UOMe $5.[1] Evidently the donor did not think much of that particular sermon! This man had an unusual way of paying tribute to his pastor.

The Scripture, however, commands us to pay a far different tribute to our pastors. In Hebrews 13, we learn that this honor, which God wants us to attribute to our pastors, involves remembrance and obedience.

The book of Hebrews was a homily, which became a circulating epistle, to encourage Jewish Christians to endure in their Christian faith. They needed to remain faithful to their faith regardless of opposition and persecution. The writer began by focusing on the Object of their faith, the Lord Jesus Christ.

Having established Christ's superiority over all that was related to the religious life of these Jews before salvation, the writer then exhorted them to remain true to their faith in Christ: "Let us hold fast the confession of our hope without wavering, for He who promised is faithful" (Heb. 10:23). To motivate them to remain faithful, the writer walked his Jewish audience down the "Hall of Faith." He called to their attention some of their ancestors who had evidenced faith under all kinds of circumstances, and who had been able to overcome even to the point of death (Heb. 11).

Surrounded by "so great a cloud of witnesses" from the past, these first-century believers were to lay aside their weight of unbelief and look unto Jesus, "the author and finisher of our faith" (Heb. 12:1-2). Hebrews 13, the last chapter of the book, contains some practical guidelines for these believers to live out their unwavering faith in Jesus Christ.

Some of the directives in chapter 13 dealt with their conduct toward their pastors (Heb. 13:7-8, 17). The readers were to remember and to obey their leaders and be submissive to them. Compliance to these exhortations is the biblical tribute that we may pay our pastors today. Let's look at each one briefly.

The Tribute of Remembrance

The author exhorted his Jewish audience saying: "Remember those who rule over you, who have spoken the word of God to you, whose faith follow, considering the outcome of their conduct. Jesus Christ is the same yesterday, today, and forever" (Heb. 13:7-8).

We honor our pastors when we obey God's commandment to remember them. The present tense of *mnemoneuete* indicates consistency; a literal rendering is "keep on remembering," which demonstrates an ongoing obligation. "The same verb is used in 2 Timothy 2:8, where Timothy is exhorted to remember Jesus Christ."[2]

Some think that these leaders were the founders of the Hebrew church. "Although the writer is not urging the readers to dwell in the past, he is deeply conscious of the influence of the example of other men as chapter 11 shows."[3] In this verse we note two qualities about these pastors that made them worthy of remembrance.

Their Preaching

They had preached the Word of God. "These leaders probably had led the readers to Christ, because the leaders had spoken the Word to them. When you recall that few Christians then had copies of the Scriptures, you can see the importance of this personal ministry of the Word."[4]

We tend to forget pastors who have labored and sacrificed to open new fields of ministry. An evidence of their faithfulness in preaching and in their example is the group of believers they have left behind. These leaders "are placed in the same category of 'heroic examples' as the paragons of biblical history (6:12-15; 11:1-40)."[5]

Remembering our past leaders does not mean that we should always live in the past, but it does mean that we should not take for granted the blessings we received from them.

Their faith

The departed leaders also had been men of faith, a faith that was worthy of imitation. However, "The imitation which is urged upon the readers is no mechanical copying of the actions of others, but a call to emulate *their* faith."[6] The word translated "outcome" may refer to death or to leaving this life. This has led some commentators to believe that these former leaders may have been martyred. Regardless of how they had died, these leaders had been faithful to the end, just like their predecessors in the "Hall of Faith" (Heb. 11).

"Remembering, considering, and imitating the virtues of departed believers is of great spiritual importance both to one's family and to the broader family of the Body of Christ. Doing so will certainly help keep the boat afloat."[7]

Having exhorted his readers to remember their leaders, the writer then proclaims, "Jesus Christ is the same yesterday, today, and forever" (v. 8). This is a wonderfully encouraging truth; but, at first glance, it seems to be so much out of context, that it almost startles us. However, this proclamation of Christ's immutability certainly belongs with remembering past leaders (v. 7).

The author of Hebrews "has a specific reason for interjecting this confession concerning the Son's immutability. . . . With this Christological statement the author reminds his audience that the same Christ who was so real to their community in the beginning, as they were ministered to by their former leaders, presently sits in his exalted state and will rule perpetually. Although their circumstances and perspectives change, Jesus Christ and his gospel do not."[8]

Wiersbe reminds us, "Church leaders may come and go, but Jesus Christ remains the same; and it is Christ who was the center of our faith." Then Wiersbe illustrates his statement with this personal account: "After I had announced my resignation from a church I had been pastoring for several years, one of the members said to me, 'I don't see how I'm going to make it without you! I depend so much on you for my spiritual help!' My reply shocked him. 'Then the sooner I leave, the sooner you can start depending on the Lord. Never build your life on any servant of God. Build your life on Jesus Christ. He never changes.'"[9]

Pastors who have preached the gospel, which brought us to Christ, may be gone, but Jesus Christ the Lord, of whom they have spoken, remains constantly the same—the eternal, unchangeable Christ!

The Tribute of Obedience and Submission

The author of Hebrews also exhorted believers to obey their leaders: "Obey those who rule over you, and be submissive, for they watch out for your souls, as those who must give account. Let them do so with joy and not with grief, for that would be unprofitable for you" (13:17). "The writer is concerned only about attitudes and mentions two which are complementary to each other—*obey* (*peithesthe*) and *submit* (*hypeikete*) the latter word occurring only here in the New Testament."[10]

Hughes inserts an important reminder concerning this obedience and submission: "This does not mean unqualified blanket obedience—the kind that made it possible for Jim Jones to murder 800 of his followers by ordering them to drink poisoned Kool-Aid. . . . This call to obedience was never meant to entice anyone to contradict Biblical morality or individual conscience."[11]

The writer to the Hebrews set forth some motives to encourage obedience and submission to pastors, our God-appointed church leaders.

Watchful Care over the Sheep

These pastors are not tyrants. They do not lord it over the congregation but watch over (*agrypneo*) the souls of their members. *Agrypneo* literally means "to keep oneself awake" (cf. Eph. 6:18—to keep alert in prayer). Leaders worthy of obedience and submission are caring shepherds. Day and night they watch over their people, sometimes staying awake through the night praying for them, especially for those who have strayed.

The two commands *obey* and *be submissive* "involve yielding to and respecting the leaders as they give direction concerning right Christian doctrine. By guiding the church in doctrinal integrity the leaders 'watch over' (*agrypneo*) the lives of those committed to their charge."[12] This is not an easy task! "Quite frankly, it is much easier to 'win souls' than it is to 'watch for souls' (see Ezek. 3:16-21). The larger a church grows, the more difficult it becomes to care for the sheep. . . . However, when a shepherd is faithful to watch for souls, it is important that the sheep obey him."[13]

Accountability to God

Someday, all pastors will have to give an account to God for how they have carried out their responsibility:

"While all Christians will be at the Bema, professed leaders and teachers of the church will undergo a stricter judgment. So we see that the rationale for obedience was very clear for the Hebrew church. 1) Their leaders were so committed to watching over the souls under their care that they lost sleep. And 2) they were doing this with the powerfully motivating knowledge that they would answer to God for how well they did it. Such care invites obedience from God's people."[14]

Leaders will answer for their care of souls. Scriptures teach clearly that spiritual responsibility brings with it a higher level of accountability and judgment. James wrote about this principle: "Not many of you should presume to be teachers, my brothers, because you know that we who teach will be judged more strictly" (James 3:1).

Joyful Fulfillment of Ministry

Some commentators hold that the injunction "Let them do so with joy and not with grief," is addressed to the people, not to the leaders. "In other words, it is the responsibility of the church to help their leaders rule with joy and satisfaction. One way of doing this is through willing submission to their authority. The joy of our leaders in the Lord should be a motivation for submission."[15]

Others think that the injunction is addressed to the leaders: "Leaders are enjoined to perform their tasks joyfully, which would exclude an overbearing approach."[16] If the admonition is to church leaders, followers can greatly ease the burden of their leadership. "Consequently, instead of working against them the members of the congregation are to yield to their leaders so that their ministry may be carried out with 'joy.'"[17]

Whether the injunction is to the congregation or to the leaders, it is the congregation's obedient response that makes it possible for the pastor to fulfill his ministry joyfully! Too many believers create problems and tension for their pastor by constantly complaining and resisting his authority. Cheerfulness, helpfulness, and loyalty from his members are a blessing to every pastor, enabling him to carry out his ministry joyfully!

MacArthur states that it is a severe and all too common issue for "stubborn, self-willed people in church congregations to rob their pastors of the joy God intends faithful pastors to have. Failure to properly submit brings grief rather than joy to pastors, and consequently brings grief and displeasure to God, who sends them to minister over us. . . . It is a grief often known only to the pastor, his family, and to God. Because lack of submission is an expression of selfishness and self-will, unruly congregations are not likely to be aware of, or to care about, the sorrow they cause their pastor and other leaders."[18]

When my wife would come home from pastors' wives meetings, she would often tell me about wives who were in tears as they shared their burden of some members' mistreatment of their husbands. The conflict may be between the pastor and a deacon who may oppose the pastor to gain power in the church. I was a pastor for eleven years and a deacon for eighteen years, and presently serve as a deacon. I have seen both sides! The pastorate involves dealing with disobedient people, but it also includes the joy of observing obedient, submissive members as they grow under the preaching of the Word. "A pastor's sweetest joy is to see those in his church walking with the Lord and bearing fruit. And, contrarily, one of the saddest tragedies that can come to a pastor is that of spending years of his life working with those who do not grow, do not respond to spiritual leadership, and do not walk in the truth."[19]

Useless Outcome of Disobedience

The writer reminded his readers of the futility of disobedience. He said, "That would be unprofitable for you." Guthrie explains it this way: "When members of the church fail to submit themselves to the leadership, the leaders end up working under an emotional burden that gives them a life filled with sighs. Such a condition is 'of no advantage' to the congregation since ministry is diminished by undue emotional stress."[20]

Disobedience prevents learning and stunts proper spiritual growth. Constant rebellion against a pastor "brings spiritual barrenness and bitterness. A person who never brings joy will never have joy. To cause our leaders grief is harmful to ourselves as well as to them and to the church as a whole. It is unprofitable for you. When we do not have a loving and obedient spirit, God is displeased, our leaders are grieved, and we lose our joy as well. . . . You will never find a truly happy pastor apart from a happy congregation, or a happy congregation apart from a happy pastor."[21]

The greatest tribute we can pay to our former pastors is to remember them by following their faithful example. The best tribute we can render to our current pastor is wholehearted obedience and submission!

Endnotes

[1] Paul Lee Tan, *Encyclopedia of 7700 Illustrations,* "Pastor—Laymen," #4241 (Dallas: Bible Communications, 1979), p. 977.

[2] Donald Guthrie, *Hebrews* in *The Tyndale New Testment Commentary* (Grand Rapids: Zondervan, 1998), pp. 270-71.

[3] Ibid., p. 270.

[4] Warren W. Wiersbe, *Be Confident* (Wheaton, IL: Victor Books, 1982), p. 150.

[5] George H. Guthrie, *Hebrews* in *The NIV Application Commentary:* Hebrews (Grand Rapids: Zondervan, 1998), p. 439.

[6] Donald Guthrie, *Hebrews* in *Tyndale*, p. 271.

[7] R. Kent Hughes, *Hebrews: An Anchor to the Soul,* volume 2 in *Preaching the Word Series* (Wheaton, IL: Crossway Books, 1993), p. 227.

[8] Ibid.

[9] Wiersbe, *Be Confident*, p. 150.

[10] Donald Guthrie, *Hebrews* in *Tyndale*, p. 276.

[11] Hughes, *Hebrews*, p. 235.

[12] George Guthrie, *Hebrews* in *NIV Commentary*, p. 442.

[13] Wiersbe, *Be Confident*, pp. 151-152.

[14] Hughes, *Hebrews*, p. 442.

[15] MacArthur, *The MacArthur New Testament Commentary: Hebrews* (Chicago: Moody Press, 1983), p. 446.

[16] Donald Guthrie, *Hebrews* in *Tyndale*, p. 277.

[17] George Guthrie, *Hebrews* in *NIV Commentary*, p. 442.

[18] MacArthur, *Hebrews*, p. 447.

[19] Ibid., pp. 445-46.

[20] George Guthrie, *Hebrews* in *NIV Commentary*, p. 442.

[21] MacArthur, *Hebrews*, pp. 447-448.

Appendix B

... And What About Women?

The subject in this book has been *pastors and deacons*. However, lest some think that there is no place for women in ministry in the church, please note again chapter 13 dealing with deacons' wives—they are a vital part of their husbands' ministries. Further, any pastor who believes that women should have no part at all in ministry is overlooking the words of the Apostle Paul found in 1 Corinthians 11 when he made provision for women to pray and use their spiritual gifts in the church.

Paul makes it clear that women are not to be pastors (1 Tim. 3:2) or deacons (3:12), nor are women to teach men or usurp authority over them (2:12). However, the apostle certainly did **not** mean that women have no place in serving the Lord in the local church!

Priscilla joined her husband in helping Paul in his church planting efforts in Corinth (Acts 18:1; Rom. 16:3). The apostle commended Mary for her work in the church at Rome (Rom. 16:6). In addition, Tryphena and Tryphosa clearly ministered in the church and served well (Rom. 16:12).

As a pastor at Maranatha Baptist Church, I was pleased with the large part our ladies had in the life of the church. With God's help, my wife Martha organized the ladies' ministries. As specified by the church constitution, the pastor and deacons approved the overall women's ministry, including the bylaws. The ladies' annual business meetings were always well attended as they planned their activities for the year, and so were their quarterly meetings.

Women might serve in the following ministries, some of which had "sub-ministries": Benevolent, Bible Studies, Fellowships, Fellowship-Helpers, Missions, Nursery, Prayer Chains, Prayer Partners, and Publicity. Each new lady who joined the church was plugged into at least one area of service—the Fellowships Ministry. All the other ministries were open to any church lady who wanted to serve voluntarily.

On the following pages you will find a list of ministry activities open to women prepared by Martha. Like men, women are the recipients of spiritual gifts sovereignly distributed by the Holy Spirit (1 Cor. 12:11). Since ladies are a vital part of the local church, it will suffer if they are not allowed to exercise their gifts biblically. However, the congregation benefits greatly when lady members are given opportunities to serve (Rom. 12:3-8; 1 Cor. 12:7). Let them serve joyfully!

BIBLE STUDIES MINISTRY

MINISTRIES OPEN TO WOMEN
By Martha Hartog

God places some restrictions to women's ministries in the local church. However, many valuable ministries are open to us that conform to the guidelines in His Word (cf., 1 Tim. 2:11-15; Tit. 2:3-5). Therefore, (1) we must consider these biblical guidelines carefully before we think about serving in our local church. (2) Moreover, we must be willing to carry out these ministries under the authority of our pastor, our God-appointed leader, and not strive to promote our own agenda. (3) Finally, every aspect of our service must be done for the purpose of edifying our brothers and sisters in the Lord and for the glory of God—to image our Savior and to make Him known to others!

Homemaking, hospitality

Acts 12:12; 16:14-15; 1 Tim. 5:10; Titus 2:5; 1 Pet. 4:9

1. Managing and organizing our household
2. Hosting meals
3. Hosting Bible studies, fellowships, showers, recreational activities (craft fellowships, cookie-exchanges, slumber parties)

Praying

Eph. 6:18; 1 Thess. 5:17-18; 2 Thess. 3:1; James 5:16

1. Individually [prayer journal]
   a. For church family: their spiritual growth, physical well being
   b. The pastor, others in leadership positions (deacons, Sunday school superintendent, teachers): their needed wisdom and strength
2. Corporately
   a. Faithful attendance to prayer meetings and participation
   b. Helping coordinate prayer chains and small prayer groups for particular needs or events
   c. Helping promote special days of prayer
   d. Organizing women's prayer breakfast

Teaching

Tit. 2:3-5; Acts 18:26; Rom. 12:7

1. Teaching alone
   a. Women: Sunday school, Bible studies, devotionals
   b. Children: Sunday school, Children's church, VBS, AWANA, Joy Clubs, Kids 4Truth, sports camps
2. Team teaching with husband
   a. Youth
   b. Couples: parenting classes
   c. New believers: home Bible studies with couples
3. Writing: Sunday school and VBS curriculum, devotional books, Bible study books

Helping

Rom. 12:7a; 16:1-16; 1 Tim. 3:11; 1 Pet. 4:10-11

1. Within the church
   a. Nursery: eagerly volunteer
   b. Church functions: planning, cooking, cleaning
   c. Visitation: the elderly, the sick (at home, nursing home, hospital), absentee members
   d. Hospitality: welcoming new-comers, welcome table [setting out coffee, baking goodies],
   e. Transportation: for elderly and handicapped
   f. Audio/visuals: developing, organizing, preparing
   g. Secretarial/clerical: library, church office
   h. Writing/graphics: Internet, publicity, programs, flyers
   i. Buildings and grounds [work day]: decorating, cleaning, landscaping
   j. Childcare: for sick mothers
   k. Website
   l. Prepare ladies for baptism
   m. Ordering flowers for special occasions, the sick, and funerals
   n. Skits: writing them or participating in them

2. Under the auspices of the church
   a. Nursing home ministry: music, setting up, helping round up residents, bring treats
   b. Hospice care: volunteer, provide meals or snacks for family
   c. Tutoring: regular school subjects, English classes to immigrants
   d. Aiding the elderly and physically impaired: grocery shopping, transportation

Helping, continued

    e. Sporting events: team participant, coach, provide snacks, cheer!
    f. Crisis pregnancy care center: office work, cleaning, organizing supplies, leading Bible studies
    g. Rescue mission: helping with meals
    h. Women prisoners: Bible studies
    i. Abused women crisis center: Bible studies

Counseling
Ps. 119:24; Rom. 12:8; Gal. 6:1-2; 2 Tim. 3:16-17

1. Counseling as a team with husband: pre-marital, marriage, families [parenting]
2. Counseling alone: women and children

Missions
Acts 1:8; 18:18; Eph. 6:18-20; Phil. 4:14-19

1. Going to the mission field as a missionary
2. Communicating with missionaries: e-mail, regular mail, phone
3. Praying for missionaries
4. Giving to missions: money, supplies, care packages
5. Hosting missionaries in the home
6. Helping promote missions: special days like "Missions in October," banquets, luncheon, teas
7. Visiting the mission field

Missions, continued

8. "Adopting" missionaries
9. Sponsoring youth missions trips
10. Prayer letter ministry: sending letters for missionaries
11. Organizing teaching materials for the mission field
12. Prophet's chamber: cleaning and upkeep
13. Christmas gifts for MK's

Evangelism and Discipleship
Matt. 28:19-20; Acts 18:24-26

This two-fold ministry with women involves (1) Sharing the gospel and (2) Bible studies

1. Personal witnessing: one-on-one, giving testimony at an event
2. Ladies' Bible studies [one-on-one discipleship]
3. Visitation: newcomers, follow-up of new converts
4. Door to door canvassing
5. Counseling women and children who come forward
6. Telephone ministry: inviting unchurched people
7. Outreach to children (AWANA, Joy Clubs, VBS, Kids 4Truth, sports camps)
8. Nursing home
9. Crisis pregnancy care center
10. Abused women crisis center
11. Women prisoners
12. Rescue mission
13. Christmas teas: invite unsaved neighbors
14. Christmas cookies exchange event
15. Weight loss classes or exercise classes
16. Ladies' luncheon outreach

Giving
Rom. 12:8; 2 Cor. 9: 6-15

1. Food for needy church people: as a participant of food showers or as an individual delivering a grocery bag to someone in need
2. Clothing: clothing exchange
3. Money [besides regular tithes]: funds for the needy privately or through the benevolent offering
4. Meals for college students: planning the school year calendar, bringing food

Music
Eph. 5:18-20; Col. 3:15-17

1. Special music (solo or ensemble): instrumental, vocal
2. Choir:
   a. Adult: member, piano player
   b. Children's: director, piano player, keeping the children in line
   c. Patch the Pirate leader or helper: music or drama
3. Training/music lessons: instrumental, vocal
4. Composition
5. Ordering choir music and keeping it organized
6. Helping with the music schedule: contacting people
7. Caroling
8. Drama for special music events: Easter, Christmas

Scripture
References

Scripture References

Chapter & Verse	Page
Genesis	
28	134
Psalms	
23:2	144
111:10	89
119:53	37
119:89	13
Proverbs	
1:7	89
18:22	58
Ezekiel	
3:16-21	172
Matthew	
11:29	46
16:18	161
18:15-20	152
19:18	73
20:26	82
25:21	73, 160
Mark	
10:45	88
John	
10:1-30	73
10:3	144
10:11-12	144
10:11	145
20:17-28	139
21:15-17	73

Chapter & Verse	Page
Acts	
4:4	158
4:13	135
6:1-8:40	79
6	77,78,79,81,87,93,158
6:1-8	78,79
6:1-6	78
6:1-4	158
6:1	77
6:2	77
6:3	87,88,89,156
6:5	78, 89
7	89
7:59	135
8:5ff	135
11	30
14	30
15	30
16	30
18:1	179
20	30
20:1	139
20:2	140
21	30
22	30
20:17-28	139
20:17	140
20:28	140
21:7	159
Romans	
7:3	59
12:2	67
12:3-8	180
12:7	66
13:4	82
13:12-14	43
15:8	82
16	113
16:1	82,115,116

Scripture References (Cont.)

Chapter & Verse	Page
Romans Cont.	
16:1-2	115
16:3	179
16:6	116,179
16:12	116,179
1 Corinthians	
3:5	82
7:2	59
9:14	152
9:25	71
11	179
11:21	38
12	150
12:7	180
12:11	180
12:28-29	66
2 Corinthians	
3:6	82
5:10	72
10:2	46
Galatians	
5:16	88
5:22-23	46, 88
Ephesians	
3:7	82
3:12	135
4	30
4:11-12	147
4:11	66
\4:12-13	147, 149
4:15	39
4:17-32	43
5:18	88

Chapter & Verse	Page
Ephesians Cont.	
5:25	161
6:18	172
6:21	82
Philippians	
1	30
1:1	82
2:1-8	88
2:3	23
4:2	113,116
4:3	116
Colossians	
3:5-17	43
1 Thessalonians	
2:19	71
5:12-13	135,153
1 Timothy	
1:15	49
1:19-20	103
2:9	113
2:10	113
2:11	113
2:12	113,115, 179
2:14	113
3	29,30,43,56,69,83,84,87,101, 116,156,161
3:1-12	158
3:1	49
3:2	31,43,44,53,60,61,65, 66,102, 106,113,122, 130,140,179
3:3	35,37, 38,39,46,157
3:4-5	146
3:4	55,56,60,122.125
3:5	54,122,125,148
3:6-7	128
3:6	32,34
3:7	68,113

Scripture References (Cont.)

Chapter & Verse   *Page*

1 Timothy Cont.
3:8-13	93,114,122
3:8	35,93,94,97,101,108, 111,114,128
3:9	103,105
3:10	104,105,106,121
3:11	109,110,111,113,114,117,121 122,127,128,130,131
3:12	110,111,113,118, 121 121,122, 125,179
3:13	133
3:15	69,161
4:9	49
5:9	113
5:14	58,117
5:17-18	152
5:19-20	152

2 Timothy
2:2	142
2:11	49
2:8	169
2:24-25	46
3:3	127
3:16-17	17
3:19	48
4:2	142
4.8	71
4:13	142

Chapter & Verse   *Page*

Titus
1	29,30,43,56,69
1:5	54
1:6	53,61
1:7	32,35,36,37,38,105,106
1:8	44,47,65,67
1:9	48,142
2:2	101,128
2:3	127
2:4	117
3:8	49

Hebrews
3:17	37
6:12-15	169
10:19	135
10:23	168
11	168,169,170
11:1-40	169
11:7	170
11:8	170
12:1-2	168
13	167,168
13:4	58
13.7-8	167,168,169
13:17	153,167,168,171

James
1:12	71
3:1	173
4:10	135
5	30

1 Peter
1:16	47
2:9	73
4:14	72
5	30
5:1-4	139,147
5:1	29,73

Scripture References (Cont.)

Chapter & Verse   ***Page***

1 Peter Cont.

5:2-4	73
5:3	22,31,145,147
5:4	71
5:6	135

2 Peter

1:4	72
2	30

3 John

Vv, 9-10	19

Jude

v. 3	39

Revelation

2:10	72

Selected Bibliography

Selected Bibliography

Agar, Frederick A. *Church Officers*. New York: Fleming H. Revell, 1918.

_____. *The Deacon at Work*. Chicago: The Judson Press, 1923.

*Arndt, William F. and F. Wilbur Gingrich. *A Greek-English Lexicon of the New Testament and other Early Christian Literature*. 4th Revised Edition. Chicago: University of Chicago Press, 1952.

Arrington, French L. *Maintaining the Foundations: A Study of 1 Timothy*. Grand Rapids: Baker Book House, 1982.

Barrett, C. K. *The Pastoral Epistles* in the *New English Bible*. Oxford: Clarendon Press, 1963.

Barton, Bruce B., David R. Veerman, and Neil Wilson. *1 Timothy, 2 Timothy, Titus* in *Life Application Bible Commentary*. Wheaton, IL: Tyndale House Publishers, 1993.

_____. Mark Fackler, Linda K. Taylor, and Dave Veerman. *1 and 2 Peter, Jude* in *Life Application Bible Commentary*. Wheaton IL: Tyndale House Publishers, 1995.

Bassler, Jouette M. *1 Timothy, 2 Timothy, Titus* in *Abingdon New Testament Commentaries*. Nashville: Abingdon Press, 1996.

Blaiklock, E. M. *The Pastoral Epistles.* Grand Rapids: Zondervan Publishing House, 1972.

Briley, C. P. *The Deacon's Life and His Wife.* Chapel Hill, NC: No Publisher, 1962.

Burroughs, P. E. *Honoring the Deaconship.* Revised. Nashville: The Sunday School Board of the Southern Baptist Convention, 1936.

Calvin, John. *Commentaries on the Epistles to Timothy, Titus, and Philemon.* Grand Rapids: William B. Eerdmans Publishing Company, 1948.

_____. *The Epistle of Paul the Apostle to the Hebrews and the First and Second Epistles of St. Peter* in *Calvin's Commentaries.* Grand Rapids: William B. Eerdmans Publishing Company, 1963.

Campbell, Earnest R. *A Commentary of First Timothy.* Silverton, OR: Canyonview Press, 1983.

*Cedar, Paul, Kent Hughes, and Ben Patterson. *Mastering the Pastoral Role.* Portland, OR: Multnomah Press, 1991.

Chrysostom. "1 Timothy 3:12" in *Ancient Christian Commentary on Scripture: New Testament IX: Colossians, 1-2 Thessalonians, 1-2 Timothy, Titus, Philemon.* Peter Gorday, Editor. Downers Grove, IL: InterVarsity Press, 2000.

Cobb, J. E. *Cobb's Baptist Church Manual.* Revised Edition. Little Rock, AR: Baptist Publications Committee of the Baptist Missionary Association of America, 1972.

Conrad, Omar Gregory. "A Teacher's Manual for the Book of First Timothy." MABS Thesis, Dallas: Dallas Theological Seminary, 1977.

Cyril of Jerusalem. "1 Timothy 3:2b" in *Ancient Christian Commentary on Scripture: New Testament IX: Colossians, 1-2 Thessalonians, 1-2 Timothy, Titus, Philemon*. Peter Gorday, Editor. Downers Grove, IL: InterVarsity Press, 2000.
Davies, Margaret. *The Pastoral Epistles*. Sheffield, England: Sheffield Academic Press, 1996.
Dawson, David Miles. *More Power to the Preacher*. Grand Rapids: Zondervan Publishing House, 1956.
Dykes, J. Oswald. *The Christian Minister and His Duties*. Edinburgh: T. & T. Clark, 1909.
Easton, Burton Scott. *The Pastoral Epistles*. New York: Charles Scribner's Sons, 1947.
Ellicott, C. J. *A Critical and Grammatical Commentary on the Pastoral Epistles*. London: Parker, Son, and Bourn, West Strand, 1861.
*Erdman, Charles R. *The Pastoral Epistles of Paul*. Philadelphia: Westminster Press, 1928.
Fee, Gordon D. *1 and 2 Timothy, Titus* in the *New International Biblical Commentry*. Peabody, MA: Hendrickson Publishers, 1995.
Ferguson, Everett. *Backgrounds of Early Christianity*. Grand Rapids: William B. Eerdmans Publishing Company, 1993.
Fetterhoff, Dean. *The Making of a Man of God.* Winona Lake, IN: BMH Books, 1976.
Fremont, Carson K. *The qualifications, Training and Use of New Testament Deacons*. No Place: No Publisher, No Date.
Getz, Gene A. *A Profile for a Christian Life Style.* Grand Rapids: Zondervan Publishing House, 1978.
†Gillespie, G. K. *The Englishman's Greek Concordance of the New Testament*. 9th Edition. London: Samuel Bagster & Sons, 1903.

Gorday, Peter, Editor. *Ancient Christian Commentary on Scripture: New Testament IX: Colossians, 1-2 Thessalonians, 1-2 Timothy, Titus, Philemon.* Downers Grove, IL: InterVarsity Press, 2000.

Greene, J. P. *The Pastoral Epistles: 1st and 2nd Timothy, Titus.* Nashville: TN: Sunday School Board, Southern Baptist Convention, 1915.

Greene, Oliver B. *The Epistles of Paul the Apostle to Timothy and Titus.* Greenville, SC: The Gospel Hour, 1964.

*Griffith, Earle G. *The Pastor as God's Minister.* Schaumburg, IL: Regular Baptist Press, 1977.

Griffiths, Michael. *Timothy and Titus.* Grand Rapids: Baker Book House, 1996.

Gromacki, Robert G. *Stand True to the Charge: An Exposition of 1 Timothy.* Grand Rapids: Baker Book House, 1982.

Grudem, Wayne. *1 Peter* in *The Tyndale New Testament Commentaries.* Grand Rapids: William B. Eerdmans Publishing Company, 1988.

Guthrie, Donald. *Hebrews* in *The Tyndale New Testament Commentaries.* Grand Rapids: William B. Eerdmans Publishing Company, 1998.

Guthrie, George H. *The Pastoral Epistles: An Introduction and Commentary.* Grand Rapids: William B. Eerdmans Publishing Company, 1957.

_____. *Hebrews* in *The NIV Application Commentary.* Grand Rapids: Zondervan Publishing House, 1998.

Gutzke, Manford George. *Plain Talk on Timothy, Titus, and Philemon.* Grand Rapids: Zondervan Publishing House, 1978.

Hanson, A. T. *The Pastoral Epistles* In *The New Century Bible Commentary.* Grand Rapids: William B. Eerdmans Publishing Company, 1982.
Hartog, John II. *The Biblical Qualifications of a Pastor.* Ankeny, IA: Immanuel, 1992.
Hauck, Gary L. *Consistent Living: Titus & Philemon.* Schaumburg, IL: Regular Baptist Press, 1997.
Hiebert, D. Edmond. *1 Peter.* Winona Lake, IN: BMH Books, 1992.
_____. *First Timothy.* Chicago: Moody Press, 1957.
_____. *Titus and Philemon.* Chicago: Moody Press, 1957.
Hillyer, Norman. *1 and 2 Peter, Jude* in *The New International Biblical Commentary.* Peabody, MA: Hendrickson Publishers, 1992.
Hoste, William. *Bishops, Priests, and Deacons.* Kilmarnock, Great Britain: John Ritchie Publishers, No Date.
House, H. Wayne. *The Role of Women in Ministry Today.* Grand Rapids: Baker Book House, 1995.
*Howell, R. B. C. *The Deaconship: Its Nature, Qualifications, Relations, and Duties.* Valley Forge, PA: The Judson Press, n. d.
Hughes, R. Kent, and Bryan Chapell. *1 & 2 Timothy and Titus: to Guard the Deposit.* Wheaton IL: Crossway Books, 2000.
_____. *Hebrews: An Anchor to the Soul,* vol. 2, in *Preaching the Word* Series. Wheaton IL: Crossway Books, 1993.
Ironside, H. A. *Addresses on the First and Second Epistles of Timothy, also Lectures on the Epistle to Titus.* New York: Loizeaux Brothers, 1947.

Jackson, Paul R. *The Doctrine and Administration of the Church.* Schaumburg, IL: Regular Baptist Press, 1980.

Jensen, Irving L. *1 & 2 Timothy and Titus: a Self-Study Guide.* Chicago: Moody Press, 1973.

Johnson, Luke Timothy. *Letters to Paul's Delegates, 1 Timothy, 2 Timothy, Titus,* in *The New Testament in Context.* Valley Forge, PA: Trinity Press, 1996.

Kelly, J. N. D. *A commentary on the Pastoral Epistles.* Grand Rapids: Baker Book House, 1981.

Kent, Homer A., Jr. *The Pastoral Epistles: Studies in I and II Timothy and Titus.* Revised Edition. Winona Lake, IN: BMH Books, 1995.

Knight, George W. III. *Commentary on the Pastoral Epistles* in the *New International Greek Testament Commentary.* Grand Rapids: William B. Eerdmans Publishing Company, 1992.

*Lea, Thomas D. and Hay P. Jr. Griffin. *1, 2 Timothy, Titus,* in *The New American Commentary.* Nashville: Broadman Press, 1992.

Lee, Mark W. *The Minister and His Ministry.* Grand Rapids: Zondervan Publishing House, 1960.

Liddon, H. P. *Explanatory Analysis of St. Paul's First Epistle to Timothy.* Minneapolis: Klock & Klock Christian Publishers, 1978.

Liefield, Walter L. *1 & 2 Timothy, Titus* in *The NIV Application Commentary.* Grand Rapids: Zondervan Publishing House, 1999.

Litfin, A. Duane. "1 Timothy" in *The Bible Knowledge Commentary, New Testament Edition.* John F. Walvoord and Roy B. Zuck, Editors. Wheaton, IL: Victor Books, 1983.

Lightner, Robert P. "Philippians" in *The Bible Knowledge Commentary, New Testament Edition*. John F. Walvoord and Roy B. Zuck, Editors. Wheaton, IL: Victor Books, 1983.

Longenecker, Harold L. *Building Town & Country Churches*. Chicago: Moody Press, 1973.

MacArthur, John. *I Timothy* in *The MacArthur New Testament Commentary*. Chicago: Moody Press, 1995.

_____. *Hebrews* in *The MacArthur New Testament Commentary*. Chicago: Moody Press, 1983.

McGee, J. Vernon. *1 & 11 Timothy, Titus, Philemon*. Pasadena, CA: Thru the Bible Books, 1978.

McKnight, Scot. *1 Peter* in *The NIV Application Commentary*. Grand Rapids: Zondervan Publishing House, 1999.

McLachlan, Douglas R. "The Marks of Leadership: 1Timothy 3:1-7." Minneapolis: Class Notes, Central Baptist Seminary, 1986.

McNamara, Roger N. and Ken Davis. *The YBH Handbook of Church Planting*. No Place: Xulon Press, 2005.

*Meisinger, George E. *The Local Church and Its Leadership*. Revised Edition. Minnetonka, MN: Maranatha Baptist Church, 1975.

Moellering, H. Armin. *1 Timothy, 2 Timothy, Titus* in the *Concordia Commentary*. Saint Louis: Concordia Pulishing House, 1970.

Moody, Jess C. *You Can't Lose For Winning: A Candid Look at Minister, Layman and Church in a Changing World*. Grand Rapids: Zondervan Publishing House, 1965.

*Moulton, James Hope and George Milligan. *The Vocabulary of the Greek Testament Illustrated from the Papyri and Other Non-literary Sources.* Grand Rapids: William B. Eerdmans Publishing Company, 1930.

Mounce, Robert H. *Pass it On: First and Second Timothy.* Glendale, Cal: G. L. Regal Books, 1979.

Naylor, Robert E. *The Baptist Deacon.* Nashville, TN: Broadman Press, 1955.

Nichols, Harold. *The Work of the Deacon and Deaconess.* Valley Forge, PA: The Judson Press, 1964.

Norris, David A. *Congregational Harmony: A Manual for Deacons and Church Workers.* Revised Edition. Ames, IA: Church Strengthening Ministries, 1984.

O'Donnell, J. D. *Handbook for Deacons.* Nashville: Randall House Publications, 1973.

Ogilvie, Lloyd J. *Acts* in *The Communicator's Commentary.* Waco, TX: Word Books, 1983.

Oxford Dictionary of the Christian Church. F. L. Cross, Editor. Oxford: Oxford University Press, 1997.

Plummer, Alfred. *The Pastoral Epistles.* New York: George H. Doran Company, No Date.

Rice, John R. *God's Work: How to Do It.* Murfreesboro, TN: Sword of the Lord, 1971.

Richards, Larry. *Pass it On; Our Heritage from the Apostolic Age: Studies in 1 and 2 Timothy, Titus, 1 and 2 Peter, Jude, 1, 2, and 3 John.* Elgin, IL: David C. Cook Publishing Company, 1978.

Robertson, A. T. *Word Pictures in the New Testament,* Nashville: Broadman Press, 1933.

Sper, David, Editor. *How Can We Work Through Our Differences.* Grand Rapids: Resources for Biblical Communication, 1992.

*Strong, James. *The Exhaustive Concordance of the Bible*. Nashville: Abingdon-Cokesbury Presss, 1890.
Tan, Paul Lee. *Encyclopedia of 7700 Illustrations*. Dallas: Bible Communications, 1979.
Taylor, Thomas. *Exposition of Titus*. Minneapolis: Klock & Klock Christian Publishers, 1980.
Terry, Robert J. *Pastoral Leadership*. Plymouth, MN: Plymouth Baptist Church, 1974.
*Thayer, Joseph Henry. *A Greek-English Lexicon of the New Testament*. New York: American Book Company, 1889.
Theodore of Mopsuestia. "1 Timothy 3:2b" in *Ancient Christian Commentary on Scripture: New Testament IX: Colossians, 1-2 Thessalonians, 1-2 Timothy, Titus, Philemon*. Peter Gorday, Editor. Downers Grove, IL.: InterVarsity Press, 2000.
*Thomas, Donald F. *The Deacon in a Changing Church*. Valley Forge, PA: The Judson Press, 1969.
Toussaint, Stanley D. "Acts" in *The Bible Knowledge Commentary, New Testament Edition*. John F. Walvoord and Roy B. Zuck, Editors. Wheaton, IL: Victor Books, 1983.
Trentham, Charles A. *Studies in Timothy*. Nashville: Convention Press, 1959.
Vincent, Marvin R. *Words Studies in the New Testament*. Grand Rapids: William B. Eerdmans Publishing Company, 1946.
Wagner, E. Glenn and Steve Halliday. *Escape From Church, Inc*. Grand Rapids: Zondervan Publishing House, 1999.
Westing, Harold J. *Church Staff Handbook*. Revised Edition. Grand Rapids: Kregel Publications, 1997.

Wiersbe, Warren W. *Be Confident: How to Keep You Balanced in the Day We Live*. Wheaton, IL: Victor Books, 1982.

_____. *Be Faithful. Its Always too Soon to Quit! An Expository Study of the Pastoral Epistles, 1 and 2 Timothy and Titus*. Wheaton, IL: Victor Books, 1981.

Wikipedia. http://en.wikipedia.org/wiki/Clerical_celibacy. "Development of clerical celibacy in the Christian church." Accessed 2/21/2008.

_____. "Theological foundations." Accessed 2/21/2008.

Wuest, Kenneth S. *The Pastoral Epistles in the Greek New Testament for the English Reader*. Grand Rapids: William B. Eerdmans Publishing Company, 1952.

* The asterisk before several of the above books indicates that they were useful in research but were not directly quoted.

ISBN 1425162010

9 781425 162016